Cook Korean!

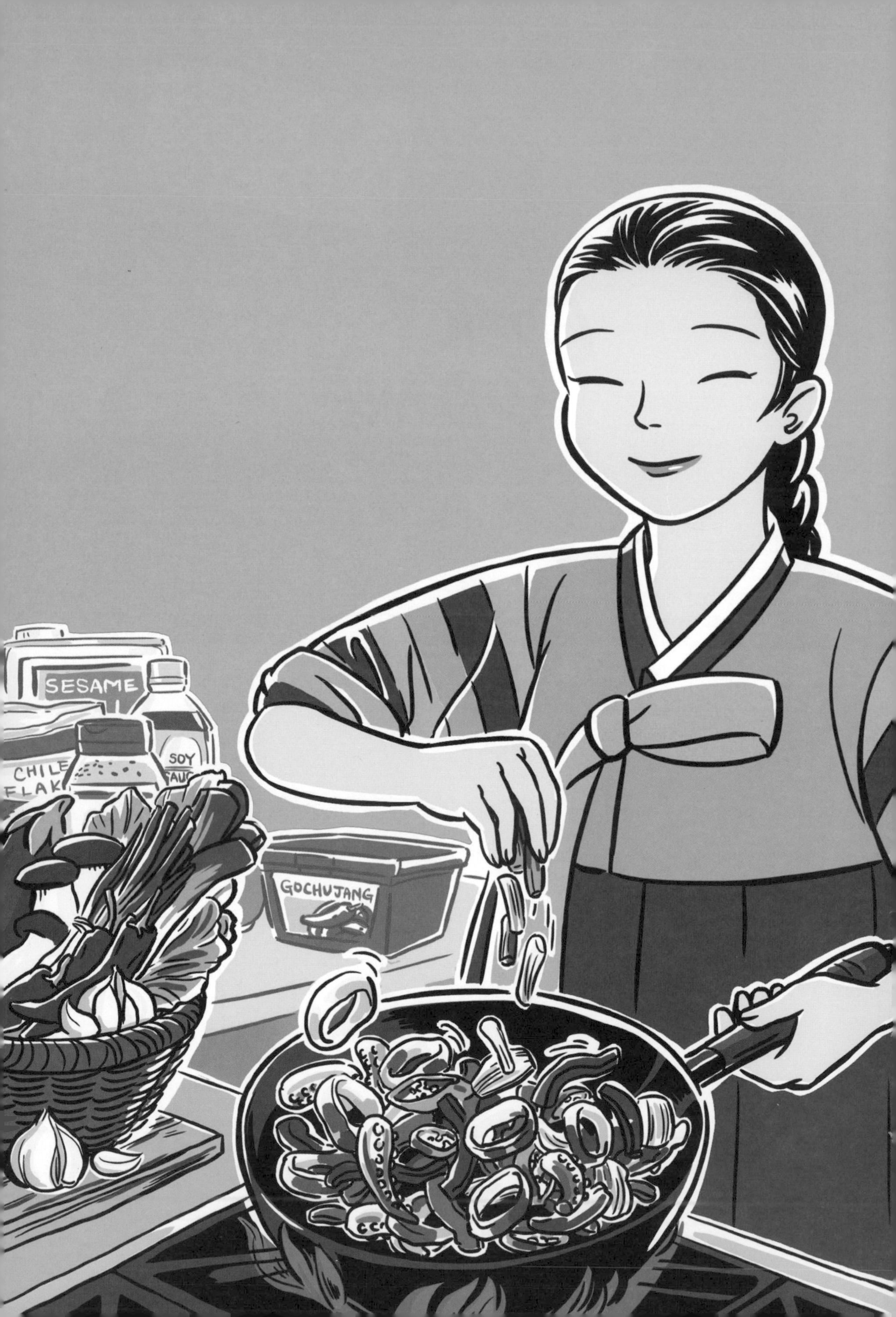
SESAME
SOY
CHILE
GOCHUJANG

A COMIC BOOK
WITH RECIPES

ROBIN HA

TEN SPEED PRESS
Berkeley

Contents

PROLOGUE

My mom was a busy working mom but she always made sure that I ate healthy homemade meals.

She made breakfast, lunch, and dinner all before I even got up for school in the morning and put them in the refrigerator for me to eat.

YAWN...
Taste
Reach
Season
Flip
CUT
WASH

When I (rarely) caught her cooking, she worked so fast that it looked like she just waved her hands and the food magically appeared on the table.

I never developed an interest in cooking because it seemed like something I would never be able to do.

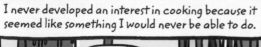

Breakfast is ready.

OK, mom.

Besides, I had other things on my mind, like reading and drawing comics.

Even when I left home for college, I didn't cook. There were cafeterias and restaurants around the school.

RAMEN RAMEN RAMEN
Tik
CUP NOO
CHE BRE

This is as far as I go with "cooking".

I was content to eat instant ramen and pizza every day. I thought I'd be able to live without ever picking up a knife.

Then I went to Italy in my senior year of college and stayed with an Italian family for two weeks to learn to speak Italian.

Benvenuta! (Welcome!)

The whole family would come home during siesta. They cooked and ate three-course meals for lunch and then took a nap.

It blew my mind. How did I live all my life without siesta?

The homestay mother took me into her kitchen to teach me how to make pasta and grill meat.

Non posso cucinare! (I can't cook!)

Non ti preoccupare. É molto facile. (Don't worry. It's very easy.)

I wanted to be part of their wonderful culture.

So I accepted the challenge.

Soon I could follow her instructions even with my broken Italian.

I realized making food was actually easy, and so much fun. And everything tasted more delicious because I helped make it.

The veil around cooking started to lift, and I slowly began to make my own meals.

For the rest of my senior year, I lived in group housing with a big communal kitchen in Rome. I learned many new recipes from my housemates.

I spent more time in the kitchen than in the studio.

After graduating from college, I moved to NYC to work as a designer and a cartoonist.

I lived in a tiny, shared apartment with a small kitchen in the East Village.

The city offered the whole world's kitchen on every corner.

UKRAINIAN RESTAURANT

FRENCH

So many choices!

I became obsessed with finding the next best food in the city. With each new dish I ate, my taste buds became more greedy, decadent, and refined.

There was no time or desire for cooking in my dingy little kitchen.

TUMBLE-WEED

My refrigerator went back to the dismal state of my freshman year of college.

A few years later, I moved out of the East Village to live in my own apartment in Brooklyn.

My new haircut

Ah, nice and quiet!

It was far away from the hustle and bustle of Manhattan, and also from all of my favorite restaurants.

All I found in my new neighborhood were mediocre Italian-American restaurants and bad fast food takeouts.

PIZZA

CHINESE

I missed the diverse and authentic food in Manhattan. Most of all, I needed good Korean food.

But an 1½-hour subway ride for every meal wasn't an option.

Out of desperation, I started asking my mom for easy Korean recipes and also looking at cookbooks and blogs.

I realized Korean food was easy to make, just like Italian food.

Not only did my homemade Korean food taste good, it was also much cheaper than going out to eat. Soon, cooking Korean food became a part of my everyday life.

Chop, throw in some sauce, then voilà! A delicious meal was served. I was hooked on the instant gratification of cooking and eating. It became my alternative creative outlet.

The joy of cooking reminded me of how I felt about drawing when I was young, without any rules or deadlines. I cooked to relax and clear my head when I got tired of comics and design work. Cooking became my meditation.

Whenever I'd bring my food to work or to picnics and potlucks, many of my non-Korean friends would ask me,

How did you make this? It's so yummy!

I was delighted to see their interest in Korean food.

But I didn't know how to explain my recipes to others.

Um . . . you just cook pork and some vegetables with soy sauce and Korean chile paste. Oh, and add some garlic and ginger too. It's so easy!

How many spoonfuls of the chile paste did you use?

Most Koreans don't measure anything while cooking. Besides, I am a cartoonist, not a chef. How could I ever teach anyone about cooking?

At the same time, I was immensely proud of Korean food and wanted to share it with everyone.

Let's make it together some time.

That would be wonderful!

Oh, can I come too?

If someone like me could make Korean food well, anyone could. I wanted every novice cook in the world to not fear making Korean food.

Then the idea came to me. Why not make a comic about cooking Korean food and put it online?

I bought measuring cups, a scale, and a timer and started the Tumblr "Banchan in Two Pages." I measured and recorded my recipes. I tweaked them over and over until I got the best versions.

When I sat down to draw the first page of the comic, a character popped into my mind.

Koreans don't really wear hanbok (Korean traditional dress) anymore, but what the heck, she is a figment of my imagination!

I named her Dengki.

While I spent all my youth drawing comics, Dengki cooked Korean food instead.

Ready when you are!

I'll let her teach while I sit back and draw.

INTRODUCTION

You're just in time for a Korean feast! Eating meals together is a huge part of Korean culture, and we share almost everything on the table. The side dishes are called banchan and there are hundreds of different kinds. My name is Dengki and I can show you how to make a lot of them.

Most Koreans eat rice and kimchi at all three meals, every day. Want to eat piping hot spicy fish soup for breakfast? Sure! You can eat any dish at any time of day in Korea.

We don't have much distinction between appetizers and main courses. We put everything on the table together!

We don't really eat desserts. At the end of a meal, we simply wash it all down with a cup of tea and a slice of fruit.

10

7 Key Ingredients
IN KOREAN COOKING

Most of these are easily found at your local Asian or organic grocery store. Or you can buy them online—hooray for modern civilization!

2) Soybean paste (doenjang)
Korean soybean paste is similar to Japanese miso paste, but it's saltier and more pungent.

1) Korean red chile flakes (gochugaru)
This is the key ingredient in kimchi, and it is responsible for Korean cuisine's spicy reputation.

3) Toasted sesame seeds (bokkeumkkae)
Toasted sesame seeds are used as a garnish to add crunchiness and nutty flavor.

4) Fish sauce (aekjeot)
Fish sauce adds the briny umami flavor in many dishes, especially kimchi. If you're vegetarian, you can substitute soy sauce for fish sauce.

5) Toasted sesame oil (chamgirum)
This fragrant oil is often added as the last touch to enhance the rich, nutty flavor Koreans call gosohanmat.

✳ Get big bottles of soy sauce and fish sauce if you intend to cook a lot of Asian food. They last forever and are widely used in all kinds of Asian cooking.

6) Soy sauce (ganjang)
There are two kinds of soy sauce in Korean cooking. Gukganjang is lighter in color. It's saltier and used in flavoring soups. Jinganjang is the all-purpose soy sauce and is darker in color and sweeter and less salty in flavor.

7) Red chile paste (gochujang)
This deep red spicy paste is also quite sweet and starchy. It is often used in making sauces.

WHAT IS IN THE KOREAN REFRIGERATOR?

When you're cooking a lot of Korean food, it's handy to have these items around.

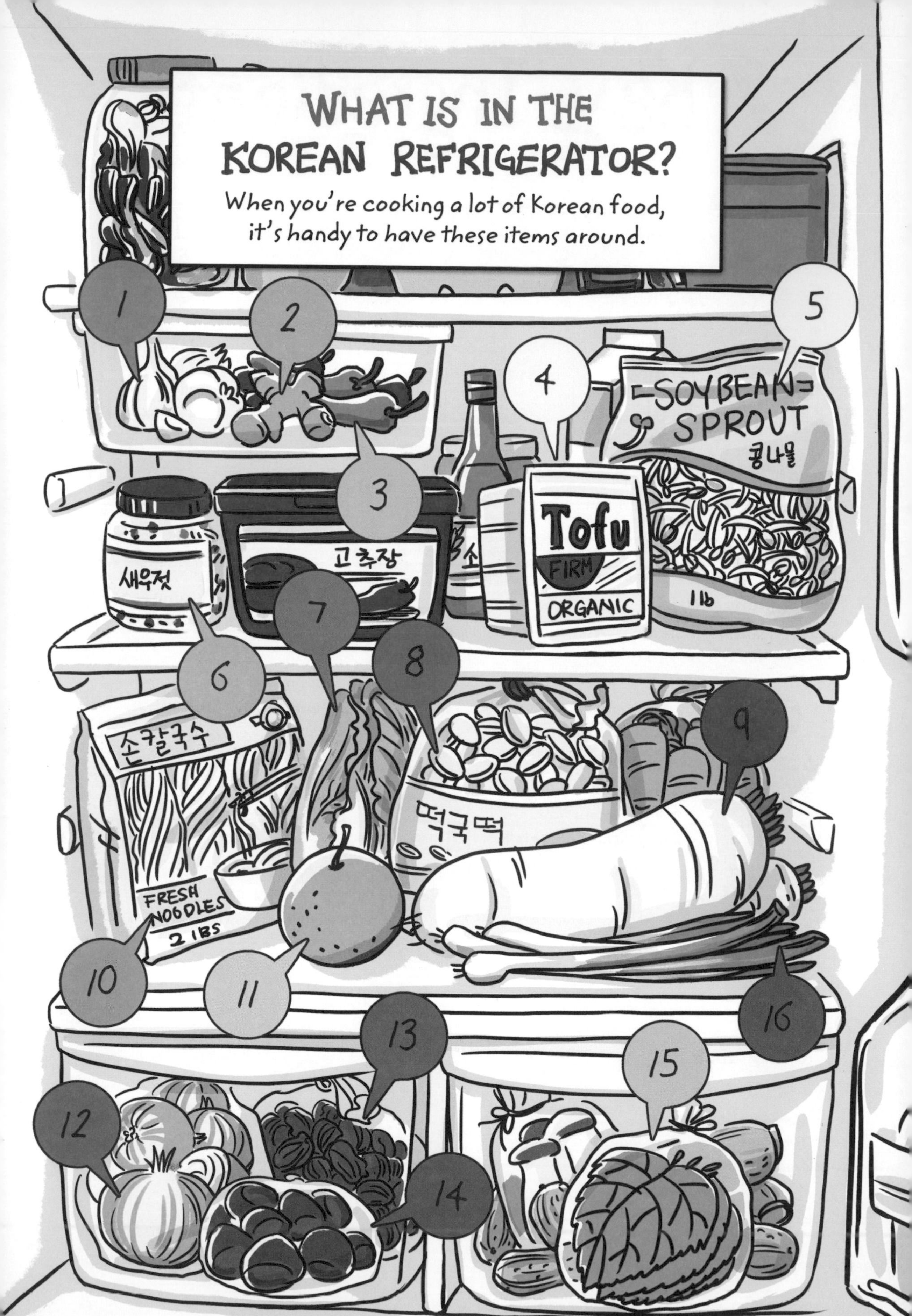
1
2
3
4
5
SOYBEAN SPROUT
콩나물
1lb
Tofu
FIRM
ORGANIC
고추장
새우젓
6
7
8
9
손칼국수
FRESH NOODLES
2 lbs
떡국떡
10
11
12
13
14
15
16

1 Garlic (manul)

Garlic is ubiquitous in Korean seasoning. You can also buy a jar of peeled and crushed garlic at Korean grocery stores.

2 Ginger (saenggang)

A small amount of minced ginger is often used in marinating meat to remove the gaminess. It is also used in making kimchi to add a fresh flavor.

3 Chile pepper (gochu)

Fresh green and red chile peppers are used to spice up many soups, side dishes, and kimchi.

4 Tofu (dubu)

Tofu is made by boiling soy milk then pressing it down. It is a versatile protein component that you can add to stir-fries and soups. It usually comes in a block form, but the soft tofu (sundubu) for soups comes in tubes.

5 Soybean sprouts (kongnamul)

Soybean sprouts are a common vegetable in simple side dishes and soups.

6 Salted fermented shrimp (saeujeot)

Tiny shrimp packed in tons of salt, it is mainly used as the salting and fermenting ingredient in kimchi making. Saeujeot tastes similar to fish sauce but with more brine and a crunchy texture.

7 Napa cabbage (baechu)

Napa cabbage is mostly used in making kimchi. It is also used to wrap boiled meats or added to soybean paste soups or pork bone soups.

8 Sticky rice cake (tteok)

Sticky rice cake is made by smashing sticky rice until it becomes goopy. The most common types are the finger-length tubular one used to make a popular spicy street food called tteokbokki and the elongated coin shaped one used in making the soup called tteokguk.

9 Daikon radish (mu)

This big white root vegetable is mildly spicy with a crunchy texture. You can make kimchi with it, put it in soups, pickle it, and braise it in soy sauce with meat or fish.

10 Fresh noodles (guksu)

There are many different types of ready-made packaged noodles in Korean grocery stores. They come in handy for making quick noodle soups. They are chewier and heartier than dried noodles.

11 Asian pear (bae)

An Asian pear is juicier and crunchier than its Western cousins. It has the enzymes to break down protein so it is often used in marinating and tenderizing meat. It is also used as a garnish in cold soups.

12 Onion (yangpa)

Onion is used often in marinating meat, flavoring kimchi, and making stocks.

15 Perilla leaves (kkaennip)

These delicate, fragrant leaves are used to wrap rice and meat and also to make kimchi.

13 Dried red date (daechu)

This sweet fruit is used to make many traditional Korean desserts and drinks.

14 Chestnuts (bam)

Chestnuts are often used to make Korean snacks and desserts.

16 Green onions (pa)

Green onion is used everywhere in Korean cooking: in kimchi, stocks, and braising meat, and also as a garnish.

the KOREAN Pantry

마른고추

Dried kelp (dashima)

Dried kelp is one of many dried seaweeds used in Korean cooking. It is thicker than miyeok and gim. It is mainly used in making broth.

Dried chiles (marungochu)

Used to spice up broths and sauces.

Korean rice liquor (soju)

Soju is a distilled clear liquor made from rice, barley, and potato. It is often used to cook meats. You can substitute sake or vodka.

Dried anchovies (myulchi)

Dried anchovies come in several sizes. The big ones are used to make broth. The small ones are used to make side dishes. Once opened, store myulchi in the fridge.

Dried shiitake mushrooms (pyogobeoseot)

Pyogobeoseot are mainly used in making broth. They are also used like regular mushrooms after being reconstituted in water. They add a savory, woodsy aroma to dishes.

표고버섯

PACIFIC SAURY

Strainer ball (mang)
This big strainer ball is used to hold the anchovies when making stock.

Sweet rice flour (chappssalgaru)
Used as a thickening agent in sauces and also for making small sticky rice balls called ongsimi.

Toasted seaweed (gim)
Gim is a thin sheet of toasted and seasoned seaweed. It is wrapped around rice and eaten like maki sushi. It is also used as a garnish to add a delicate crunch and saltiness to dishes.

Korean earthenware pot (ttukbaegi)
Ttukbaegi is a traditional unglazed earthenware pot designed to keep stews piping hot.

Dried seaweed (miyeok)
Miyeok is packaged in a long, dried bunch. Once soaked in water, it expands and becomes like green silk. It is used to make hot soups and cold side dishes and also as a wrap for rice.

Pine nuts (jat)
Pine nuts are used as a garnish and also in making sweets and porridges.

Short- or medium-grain white rice (ssal)
Cooked rice is the base of most Korean meals. You can also mix it with brown rice and other grains to make it more nutritious.

KOREAN MEAL GUIDE

This is how the typical Korean dining table looks. It could be much more elaborate, with dozens of side dishes, grilled meats, and hot pots, or it could be much simpler, with only bowls of rice, some kimchi, and a soup.

Rice is the only item that is served individually per person: the rest of the items on the table are meant to be shared. Bowls of rice come with every meal except when the main dish is a noodle or a porridge.

BAP
Cooked Rice

Rice is called ssal in Korean, and once it's cooked, it's called bap; it is the staple of Korean cuisine. The word bap also refers to the entire meal. When Koreans greet each other, we ask, "Did you have bap?"—which basically means "Did you eat?" This is how important rice is in Korean culture. Here are the four most common kinds of bap.

White rice

THE PRINCE

Hinbap or ssalbap refers to cooked rice made with only short-grain white rice like sushi rice. It is traditionally the most prized kind of bap, though less so now since it has little nutritional value. It has a soft, semi-sticky texture and a mildly sweet taste.

Barley rice

Boribap, which means barley rice, is full of nutrition and high in fiber, but it is rougher in texture and less sweet than white rice. Boribap combines barley with brown rice and white rice to enhance both the nutrition and the flavor.

Burly Barley

Bean rice

ALL BEANS WELCOME!

Kongbap is made with white rice mixed with various types of legumes, such as red beans and green peas. Fun fact: in Korea, kongbap connotes incarceration—it used to be served in jail because it cost less than white rice. But nowadays people love it as a food for wellness.

Japgokbap is a mixture of all kinds of grains and legumes, such as white, brown and black wild rice; millet; oats; lentils; black and red beans; and sometimes even pine nuts, chestnuts, and dried red dates. It is the healthiest kind of bap. Ogokbap, which is a type of japgokbap that contains five different grains, is traditionally eaten on the first full moon of the year to bring good luck.

Mixed-grain rice

RICE & ITS DELICIOUS BY-PRODUCTS

(Shungnyung)

(Nurungji)

Rice is very simple to cook, but it's also easy to mess up. Don't worry, you can make rice like a pro, too! Here is the easy way my mom taught me to make it when I was young. If you are making the multigrain version, wash the rice the day before and soak it in water overnight before cooking.

OH NOOO WHAT ARE YOU DOING!?

What? Isn't it like making pasta?

My British roommate

Nope! Here are a few things you need to do before you start boiling rice.

First!
You need a deep pot with a glass lid. (You don't need a rice cooker.)

Second: Measure the rice. 1 cup of rice grains makes 2 bowls of cooked rice.

Use short- to medium-grain white rice.

Third: Put the rice in the pot and fill it up with cold running water.

Washing the rice gets rid of excess starch so it doesn't become a glutinous goop when it's cooked.

Massage the rice to get all the cloudy dust out.

Drain the milky water and wash 3 to 5 more times, until the water is clear.

Leave enough water in the pot so it covers the rice by 1 inch. We Koreans measure it by putting a hand flat over the rice.

If the water comes just above the knuckles, it's the right amount.

Put the pot over high heat without the lid until the water starts boiling, then turn down the heat to simmer and put the lid on.

Tip: The pot shouldn't be more than halfway full of rice grains or it'll overflow.

Leave it alone and DO NOT open the lid for 15 to 20 minutes, until the water is absorbed and the rice looks fluffy. Turn off the heat and keep the lid closed for another 15 minutes.

NOW It's DONE!

If your pot doesn't have a nonstick coating, you'll find some burnt rice stuck to the bottom after you dig out all the cooked rice.

We call this nurungji. There are a couple of things you can do with it.

OR

Scrape the burnt rice from the pot and spread it out in a well-ventilated area.

Sprinkle salt and pepper on top and it'll become a tasty, crunchy snack the next day.

You can also add water to the pot and boil the burnt rice to make a savory tea called shungnyung, which is commonly drunk after a meal in Korea. (It also makes it easier to clean the pot!)

Korea's Regions & Foods

Korea is surrounded by three seas and is full of mountains. The provinces, separated by mountains and rivers developed their own strong flavors. Seafood, mountain vegetables, and fermented foods all helped Koreans get through harsh winters, and they played a huge part in the development of Korean cuisine.

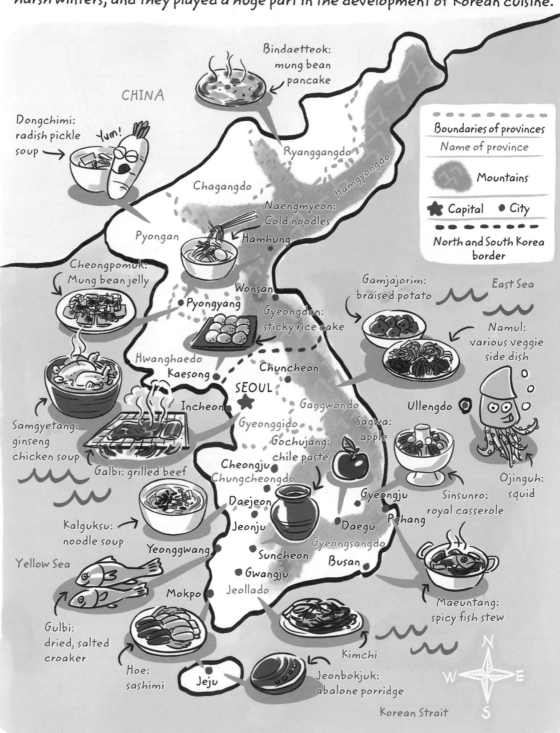

Bindaetteok: mung bean pancake

CHINA

Dongchimi: radish pickle soup → Yum!

Ryanggangdo

Chagangdo

Hamgyongdo

Naengmyeon: Cold noodles

Pyongan

Hamhung

Cheongpomuk: Mung bean jelly

Wonsan

Gamjajorim: braised potato

East Sea

Pyongyang

Gyeongdan: sticky rice cake

Namul: various veggie side dish

Hwanghaedo

Chuncheon

Kaesong

SEOUL

Samgyetang: ginseng chicken soup

Incheon

Gangwondo

Ullengdo

Gyeonggido

Sagwa: apple

Ojinguh: squid

Gochujang: chile paste

Galbi: grilled beef

Cheongju

Chungcheongdo

Gyeongju

Sinsunro: royal casserole

Daejeon

Daegu

Pohang

Kalguksu: noodle soup

Jeonju

Gyeongsangdo

Yeonggwang

Suncheon

Busan

Yellow Sea

Gwangju

Maeuntang: spicy fish stew

Mokpo

Jeollado

Gulbi: dried, salted croaker

Kimchi

Hoe: sashimi

Jeju

Jeonbokjuk: abalone porridge

Korean Strait

Legend:
- Boundaries of provinces
- Name of province
- Mountains
- ★ Capital ● City
- North and South Korea border

Dengki's Dress

Dengki is wearing a traditional Korean dress called hanbok. This particular top with striped sleeves is called saekdong jeogori, which is worn by girls on special occasions.

The silk tie at the end of her braid is called a dengki—and yes, it is where her name comes from. It was worn by young ladies who hadn't married yet. This tie let the town's bachelors know which girls were available. Once a lady got married, she turned her braid into a bun and wore an ornate pin through the bun.

I've always thought the hanbok is such a beautiful costume, but it's so uncomfortable to wear. I have no idea why the skirt has to be tied up so high, right on the breast line. Ouch!

You hardly see people wearing hanbok in Korea anymore, except on national holidays and at weddings or funerals.

Chapter 1
Kimchi and Pickles

INTRO TO KIMCHI

Kimchi is an indispensable part of any Korean meal. No matter what Koreans are eating, kimchi will always be on the table.

Kimchi is basically pickled and fermented vegetables. There are more than 100 different varieties.

The most popular types are made with napa cabbages and daikon radishes.

In Korea in late autumn, it used to be common to see the neighborhood ladies gathering to make large batches of kimchi.

They would spend a whole day turning hundreds of napa cabbages into kimchi. This tradition of collective kimchi making is called kimjang.

They packed the kimchi in giant earthenware pots called jangdok and buried them in the ground to last through the winter.

It's a natural refrigeration system!

Jangdok

Sadly, it's rare to see kimjang anymore. Modern Koreans don't have time to make giant batches of kimchi or space to store them.

Most Koreans these days think:

Why bother making kimchi when you can just buy it at the supermarket?

It was only when I moved to a place where I couldn't easily buy kimchi that I started making my own.

Koreatown, Manhattan

90 minute subway ride.

DARN!

Bay Ridge, Brooklyn

At first, making kimchi seemed like such a daunting task. But in desperation, I snapped out of my fear and got to work.

I've got nothing to lose—

except a few cabbages and an hour of my time!

Soon, I realized it wasn't difficult at all.

This was so worth it!

Yum!

Kimchi making is a simple process with three steps:

STEP 1
Salt the vegetable.

STEP 2
Add flavor to the vegetable.

STEP 3
Ferment the vegetable.

All kimchi starts with salting the vegetable. Salt draws out the water from the vegetable and makes the texture crunchier.

I'll protect you, LACTO Princess!

OH THANK YOU!

SALT

LACTIC ACID

Bad bacteria!

It also helps lactic acid-producing bacteria thrive; these promote balanced fermentation.

The three basic kimchi flavorings are:

Korean red chile flakes

Garlic

Ginger

The red color and spiciness that we automatically associate with kimchi come from the Korean red chiles.

Yup, that's me. Am I hot enough for ya?

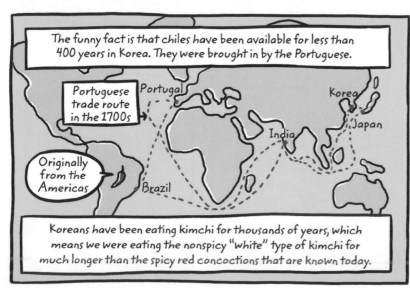

The funny fact is that chiles have been available for less than 400 years in Korea. They were brought in by the Portuguese.

Portugal

Korea

Portuguese trade route in the 1700s

Japan

India

Originally from the Americas

Brazil

Koreans have been eating kimchi for thousands of years, which means we were eating the nonspicy "white" type of kimchi for much longer than the spicy red concoctions that are known today.

Can you imagine Korean food without red chiles?

What on earth is this?

Portuguese Jesuit priest

I don't know. It burns my mouth but I like it!

Seafood adds a deep briny flavor to kimchi.

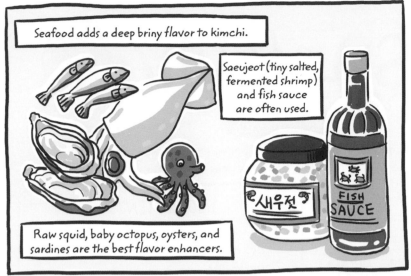

Saeujeot (tiny salted, fermented shrimp) and fish sauce are often used.

새우젓

FISH SAUCE

Raw squid, baby octopus, oysters, and sardines are the best flavor enhancers.

What distinguishes kimchi from other pickles is the fermentation process.

Push it real good!

Kimchi vegetables must be tightly packed, submerged in their juice, and the jar has to stay closed so no air gets in during fermentation.

OOPS!

Oxygen

Uh oh, the oxy-zombies!

weee

We're done for!

Probiotics

Basically, you have to maintain a safe environment for the probiotics (aka the lactic acid–forming bacteria) to do their thing.

Fermentation temperature is usually room temperature. Fermentation time and storage time vary depending on the vegetables.

Lactic Sauna

I can't stand it anymore!

70°F

Really? I'm just getting started.

When you see tiny bubbles forming in the kimchi juice, the initial fermentation is done. It's ready to eat!

Pss..

Store it in the refrigerator.

Vinegar is not used in kimchi, yet the fermented kimchi tastes tangy. It's because of the lactic acid naturally produced by the probiotics.

Every stage of kimchi has its own charm. Fresh kimchi is crunchy, spicy, and garlicky.

ALL its STINKY Goodness!

Aged kimchi is softer and tangier, the spiciness mellowed out and the juice more effervescent.

Common traditional kimchi are made with napa cabbages, daikon radishes, perilla leaves (note Korean perilla is not the same as Japanese perilla), chives, mustard greens, and cucumbers. But you can also experiment with nontraditional ingredients like tomatoes, brussels sprouts, and beets, or even fruits like watermelon, pears, apples, and peaches.

Getting inspired now? Let's make some kimchi!

easy Kimchi

(Mak Kimchi)

This is an easy, modified kimchi recipe for beginners. You can use more or less of the Korean red chile flakes, depending on your taste.

Prep time: **1 hour** Fermentation time: **1 day**
Makes **12 cups**

Food prep gloves highly recommended!

INGREDIENTS

4 pounds napa cabbage
1/2 cup kosher salt
2 cups water
4 green onions, green and white parts
1 (1-inch) piece fresh ginger, peeled
10 large cloves garlic, peeled
1 1/2 pounds daikon radish
1 large carrot, peeled
3/4 cup Korean red chile flakes
5 tablespoons fish sauce
3 tablespoons saeujeot
   (tiny salted fermented shrimp)
2 tablespoons sugar

FIRST:

Cut the cabbages lengthwise into quarters.

Then cut the quarters into bite-size pieces.

Second: Rinse the cabbage in cold running water, then drain. Sprinkle the salt all over the cabbage, then pour the water over it, and mix well.

Set aside for 45 minutes and toss the cabbage once in a while for even salting.

Meanwhile
Let's make the seasoning.
Cut the green onions on the diagonal.

Crush the ginger and garlic together. I like to use the butt of the knife.

26

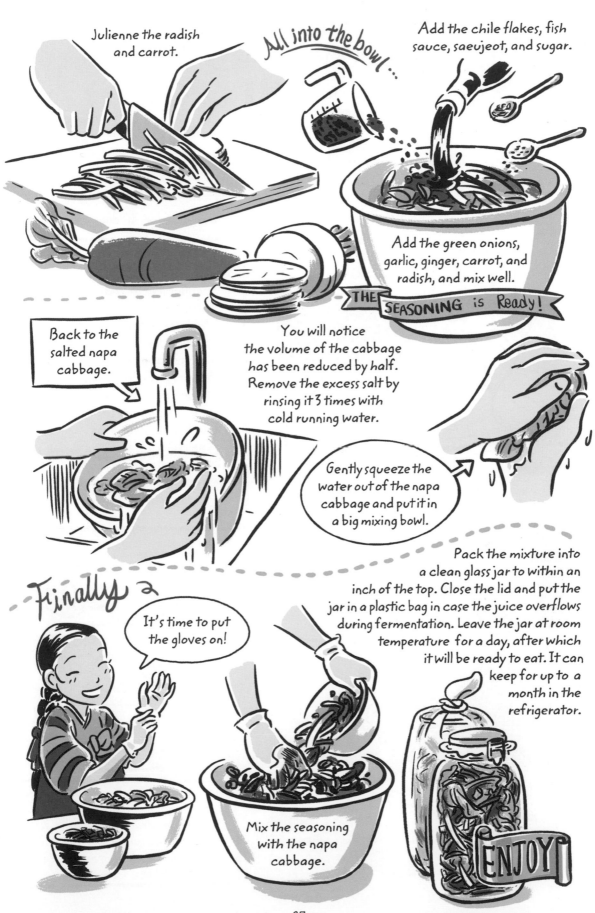

Julienne the radish and carrot.

All into the bowl...

Add the chile flakes, fish sauce, saeujeot, and sugar.

Add the green onions, garlic, ginger, carrot, and radish, and mix well.

THE SEASONING is Ready!

Back to the salted napa cabbage.

You will notice the volume of the cabbage has been reduced by half. Remove the excess salt by rinsing it 3 times with cold running water.

Gently squeeze the water out of the napa cabbage and put it in a big mixing bowl.

Pack the mixture into a clean glass jar to within an inch of the top. Close the lid and put the jar in a plastic bag in case the juice overflows during fermentation. Leave the jar at room temperature for a day, after which it will be ready to eat. It can keep for up to a month in the refrigerator.

Finally

It's time to put the gloves on!

Mix the seasoning with the napa cabbage.

ENJOY

RADISH CUBE KIMCHI
(Kkakdugi)

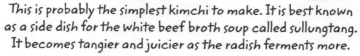

This is probably the simplest kimchi to make. It is best known as a side dish for the white beef broth soup called sullungtang. It becomes tangier and juicier as the radish ferments more.

Prep time: 1 hour 15 minutes Fermentation time: 2 days Makes 10 cups

INGREDIENTS

5 pounds daikon radish
1/2 cup kosher salt
1 tablespoon sweet rice flour
1/2 cup water
6 cloves garlic, peeled
1 1/2 inch piece fresh ginger, peeled
2 tablespoons fish sauce
1/2 cup Korean red chile flakes
2 tablespoons saeujeot
  (tiny salted fermented shrimp)
2 tablespoons sugar
5 green onions, white and
  green parts

First, wash all the dirt off the radishes and peel off any scratched or damaged areas. Then cut the radish into 1-inch cubes.

DISCARD

Put the radish cubes in a large mixing bowl and rinse it in cold running water, then drain. Sprinkle the salt all over the radish and set aside for 30 minutes. Turn it over once in a while for even salting.

Meanwhile, let's make the paste!

In a small pot, whisk the sweet rice flour into the water. Bring it to a simmer then turn off the heat.

Blend the garlic and ginger with the fish sauce.

weee

Combine the garlic, ginger, and fish sauce with the sweet rice flour paste and stir in the chile flakes, saeujeot, and sugar. Set aside for 45 minutes.

The paste is ready!

Rinse the radish cubes 3 times with cold running water to get the excess salt off, then set it aside in a strainer for 20 minutes to drain.

Chop the green onions into 1-inch pieces and add to the mixing bowl. Mix everything thoroughly by hand. Wearing food prep gloves is highly recommended!

Pack the mixture into clean glass jars and seal tightly. Leave the jars at room temperature for 2 days. It can keep for up to a month in the refrigerator.

Put the drained radish in a large mixing bowl and pour the paste on top.

ENJOY!

Cool & SPICY CUCUMBER
(Oisobagi)

This is the most popular summer kimchi in Korea.
You can substitute soy sauce for the fish sauce to make it vegan.
Prep time: 1 hour Fermentation time: 1 day Makes 8 small cucumbers

INGREDIENTS

8 small Kirby cucumbers
4 cups water
1/3 cup kosher salt
4 ounces Korean chives*
3 cloves garlic, peeled
1 large carrot, peeled
1 tablespoon sugar
1/4 cup Korean red chile flakes
1/4 cup fish sauce

*Korean chives are more delicate and garlicky than European chives.

First →

Cut the cucumbers into partial spears—leave about an inch at one end intact. Put them in a big metal mixing bowl.

Bring the water to a boil and dissolve the salt in it. Pour the hot salt water over the cucumbers and set aside for 45 minutes. This hot pickling process makes the oisobagi last longer in the refrigerator.

Now, let's make the Seasoning!

Chop the chives into pieces smaller than 1 inch, crush the garlic, and julienne the carrot.

→ Then put them all in a bowl with the sugar, chile flakes, and fish sauce.

Remove the cucumbers from the salt water and gently squeeze out any excess water.

It's time to assemble everything! Wear food prep gloves to protect your hands from the strong spices!

Pack as much seasoning as possible inside the cucumbers and put them in an airtight container. Let it ferment at room temperature for a day, then refrigerate and serve cold. It can keep for up to 10 days in the refrigerator.

Forget the Chicago dog. It's an oisobagi dog!

You can eat oisobasi the classic way with a bowl of rice.

Seriously, it goes with EVERYTHING!

To eat it fusion style, use it as pickles, in a bun with meat.

ENJOY!

GREEN ONION KIMCHI

(Pa Kimchi)

This is one of the simplest and quickest kimchis to make, and you can also use this recipe to make chive kimchi by substituting chives for green onions. Green onions are packed with vitamins and help boost the immune system, so this is a great way to add nutrition and flavor to your meals.

Prep time: 1 hour   Fermentation time: 2 days   Makes 12 cups

The type of Korean green onion used in this kimchi is called jjokpa, which is a lot thinner than regular green onions. If you can't find jjokpa, just cut regular green onions in half lengthwise to make them thinner.

Regular green onion

SPLIT

Regular green onion

Jjokpa

INGREDIENTS

3 pounds Korean green onions, white and green parts
1/2 cup fish sauce
2 tablespoons sweet rice flour
1 1/3 cup water
15 cloves garlic, peeled
1 (1/2-inch) piece fresh ginger, peeled
1 cup Korean red chile flakes
3 tablespoons sugar

→ DISCARD

Rinse the green onions and get rid of any dirt, dead leaves, and root.

DISCARD

In a mixing bowl, put the green onions root down. Pour the fish sauce over the bottom half of the green onions and soak for 30 minutes.

FISH SAUCE

Turn the green onions once in a while for even seasoning.

Meanwhile, let's make the paste!

In a small pot, whisk the sweet rice flour into the water. Bring it to a simmer, then turn off the heat.

Crush the garlic and ginger.

Combine the garlic, ginger, chile flakes and sugar with the sweet rice flour paste.

30 MINUTES LATER...

Pour the fish sauce remaining in the mixing bowl into the paste.

Food prep gloves are recommended!

Mix the paste with the green onions thoroughly by hand.

Tie 3 or 4 green onions together by their green ends. It looks pretty and it makes the onions easy to take out of the jar to serve.

Mix well, then let the paste sit for 5 minutes.

Pack the bundles of green onions into clean glass jars and seal tightly. Leave the jars at room temperature for 2 days. It can keep up to a month in the refrigerator.

ENJOY

CHAYOTE • PICKLE
(Chayote Jangachi)

WHAT'S UP!

Chayote is a vegetable that looks like a child's fist. You can find it in Asian or Latin grocery stores. Its crisp texture and mild radishlike flavor make it an excellent pickling item.

Prep time: 30 minutes Pickling time: 2 days Makes 12 cups

INGREDIENTS

4 chayotes
2 cups water
2 cups soy sauce
1 cup sugar

1 cup white vinegar
2 large yellow onions
3 jalapeños
3 cloves garlic

Quarter the chayote and cut out the seeds.

Then chop the chayote into bite-size pieces less than ½ inch thick.

Leave the skin on.

Bring the water and soy sauce to a boil, then stir in the sugar until it all dissolves.

Add the vinegar. Boil the mixture, then remove it from the heat.

Tip: Use equal parts water and soy sauce to make the brine salty enough for pickling. You can vary the amounts of vinegar and sugar, depending on your taste.

Cut the onions into bite-size chunks.

Peel the garlic.

Cut the jalapeños into rings. You can use less or more of them, depending on your taste.

Put all the vegetables into the hot soy-sugar-vinegar water. Let them sit until everything cools down.

Pack the cooled-down veggies into clean glass jars. Top off with the liquid. Make sure all of the veggies are submerged.

Store the sealed jars in the refrigerator for 2 days to develop the flavor—then it's ready to eat! It can keep for several months in the refrigerator.

ENJOY

PICKLETOPIA
NOW YOU CAN PICKLE ANYTHING!

You can use this recipe to make many other pickles. Just substitute other vegetables like garlic, cauliflower, broccoli, or asparagus for the chayote.

SQUARE-CUT KIMCHI
GAZPACHO
(Nabak Kimchi)

The best part about this watery kimchi is its tangy, refreshing broth, which gets fizzier as it ages. The little bit of Korean red chile flakes used in this recipe is more for color than for spicy flavor. Note: you will need a teabag for this recipe.
Prep time: 45 minutes Fermentation time: 2 days Makes 12 cups

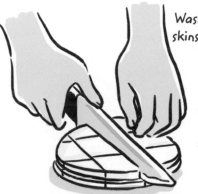

Wash and peel the outer skins of the radishes and cut them into 1 inch squares that are 1/8 inch thick.

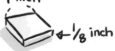

1 inch

1/8 inch

This thin square cut is called nabak in Korean, which gives this kimchi its name.

Cut the cabbage into pieces about the same size.

INGREDIENTS

1 pound daikon radish
1 1/2 pounds napa cabbage
3 tablespoons kosher salt
2 tablespoons Korean red chile flakes
5 cups water
1 small yellow onion
3 green onions, white and green parts
1 medium carrot, peeled
1 fresh red chile (optional)
1 tablespoon sweet rice flour
6 cloves garlic, peeled
1 (1/4-inch) piece fresh ginger, peeled
1 teaspoon fish sauce
2 tablespoons sugar
Asian pear, thinly sliced, for garnish
Pine nuts, for garnish

Put the radish and cabbage squares into a big mixing bowl and rinse them in cold running water, then drain. Sprinkle the salt all over and leave for 30 minutes. Turn once in a while for even salting.

Meanwhile, put the chile flakes in an empty tea bag and soak it in 4 cups of water to allow the red color to leach out into the water.

You can also use a piece of cheesecloth or a coffee filter instead of a tea bag.

Soak it for 30 minutes.

Now you've got 30 minutes to kill! Let's make the seasoning.

Halve the yellow onion. Then cut it into thin slivers and the green onions into 3-inch pieces. Julienne the carrot.

Cut the chile into thin rings if you want to make it spicy.

The paste

In a small pot, whisk the sweet rice flour into the remaining 1 cup of water.

Bring it to a simmer, then turn off the heat.

wee...

Blend the garlic, ginger, and fish sauce in a food processor...

... and add it to the sweet rice flour paste.

Everything Together!

Add the carrot, onion, green onions, sugar, and chile to the mixing bowl with the salted radish and cabbage and pour in the sweet rice flour paste.

Do not discard the brine from the radish and the cabbage. Mix it all together!

Pack the mixture into clean glass jars and top off with the pink water you made with the chile flake tea bag.

Seal the jars tightly and leave at room temperature for 2 days, then store in the refrigerator for up to a month.

Serve it chilled like gazpacho with thin slices of Asian pear and a few pine nuts for garnish!

ENJOY

Chapter 2
Vegetable Side Dishes

INTRO TO DOSIRAK

YAY! ~RRRRING!!! LUNCH TIME!

Most Korean students bring homemade lunch instead of buying lunch at the cafeteria.

Friends eat together and share each other's side dishes. Opening our lunch boxes and checking out the side dishes was the highlight of my school days.

Hmm, what do we have here?

Awesome! My mom packed the chile pickles, my favorite!

I hope Mom packed some salty beef today.

Korean lunch boxes are called dosirak.

Little compartments for the side dishes

Utensil compartment

The Thermos to keep the rice warm.

Korean side dishes are perfect for lunch boxes because they don't spoil easily and they also taste great at room temperature.

The most common side dishes for dosirak are the assortment of blanched and salted vegetables called namul and, of course, kimchi.

Sometimes I wouldn't like the side dish in my dosirak.

Man, salty beef again?

Ugh, I hate eggplant!

But there was no need to fret.

Yoink!

Because I could always trade with friends in the same predicament!

bean Sprout SALAD

(Kongnamul Muchim)

Namul is a simply prepared vegetable side dish, and there are hundreds of different varieties. They are the humble yet nutritious staple of Korean cuisine. Kongnamul is one of the most common namul and it can be used as a part of the popular rice bowl dish called bibimbap (see page 50).

Cooking time: 15 minutes   Makes 2 cups

INGREDIENTS

12 ounces soybean sprouts
1 cup water
1 teaspoon salt
1 green onion, white and
    green parts
1 clove garlic, peeled
1 tablespoon toasted sesame oil
2 teaspoons soy sauce
1 teaspoon toasted sesame seeds
Korean red chile flakes (optional),
    for serving

> Soybeans are one of the building blocks of Korean cuisine. Not only do we make soy sauce, soybean paste, and tofu with them, we also make side dishes and soups with the sprouts.

DISCARD any brown bean sprouts.

Then rinse the sprouts with cold running water.

Put the sprouts in a pot and add the water and the salt. Cover, bring it to a boil, and cook for about 7 minutes.

Cool the bean sprouts with cold running water, then drain.

& CHOP CHOP!

Gently squeeze out as much water as you can from the bean sprouts and put them in a mixing bowl.

Finely chop the green onion and mince the garlic.

Gently mix the green onion, garlic, sesame oil, soy sauce, and sesame seeds in with the sprouts.

ALL into the Bowl

If you like it spicy, add chile flakes to taste.

♥ Let's eat ! ♥

Serve warm or chilled.

ENJOY

It Makes You STRONG!
Soy Spinach
(Sigeumchi Namul)

This simple and yummy side dish packs a nutritional punch. It is great to serve with Western dishes as well as with other Korean dishes such as bibimbap (page 50) and gimbap (page 142).

Cooking time: 15 minutes   Makes 1 cup

INGREDIENTS

1 bunch spinach
Salt
1 tablespoon soybean paste
1 clove garlic, minced
1 tablespoon toasted sesame oil
Toasted sesame seeds, for garnish

WASH the spinach and remove the roots and dead leaves.

Add a pinch of salt to a big pot of water and heat to a simmer.

Blanch the spinach for about 20 seconds.

Cool the spinach with cold running water.

Gently squeeze to get as much water out of the spinach as possible and put it in a mixing bowl.

Soybean paste is the source of the umami flavor in many Asian dishes. It's also packed with amino acids, vitamins, and probiotics.

SOYBEAN

Add the soybean paste, garlic, and toasted sesame oil to the spinach.

I think food mixed by hand tastes much better! Koreans call it sonmat, or taste of the hand. (Don't forget to wear food prep gloves.)

Sprinkle some toasted sesame seeds on top and it's ready to eat!

This Recipe ♡

ENJOY

can be used to create other simple and healthy vegetable dishes by substituting other leafy greens like Swiss chard, kale, cabbage, bok choy, turnip, or collard greens for the spinach. It's a tasty way to stock up on vitamins and minerals! Just keep in mind that it takes more time to blanch thicker, tougher greens.

Can you imagine eating all of these greens in one day? With this recipe, YOU CAN!

STEAMED Asian eggplant
(Gaji Namul)

The Asian eggplant has thinner, lighter-colored skin and tastes sweeter and more delicate than its Western cousin.

Cooking time: 20 minutes
Makes 3 cups

INGREDIENTS

2 large Asian eggplants
1 green onion, white and
 green parts
1 clove garlic, peeled
1 (1/4-inch) piece fresh ginger,
 peeled
2 tablespoons soy sauce
1 tablespoon toasted sesame oil
1 teaspoon sugar
Korean red chile flakes
 (optional)
Toasted sesame seeds, for serving

First!

Get a Steamer Basket.

Cut the eggplant into 2-inch logs, then cut the logs in half lengthwise.

Pour about 2 cups of water in a pot and place a steamer in it.

Put the eggplant on the steamer.

Close the lid and steam the eggplant over high heat for 10 to 15 minutes, until it becomes soft.

Take the eggplant out of the steamer and transfer it to cool in a bowl.

Meanwhile...

Let's make the sauce. Thinly slice the green onion and mince the garlic and ginger.

Combine the soy sauce, sesame oil, sugar, garlic, ginger, and green onion. If you want it spicy, add chile flakes to taste.

THE ULTIMATE SAUCE

This sauce goes well with any vegetable.

Split the cooled eggplant logs into 2 or 3 pieces with your hands.

All into the bowl!!

Sprinkle some toasted sesame seeds on top, and it's ready to serve!

Gently stir the sauce with the eggplant until evenly cooled.

ENJOY

45

Pan-fried TOFU

(Dubu Buchim)

This is one of the easiest and tastiest ways to eat tofu and it's a great side dish to make when you're strapped for time but still want to eat healthy.

Cooking time: **15 minutes** Makes 2 cups

INGREDIENTS

1 (1-pound) package firm tofu
1 tablespoon olive oil
1 green onion, white and green parts
4 teaspoons soy sauce
2 teaspoons rice vinegar
1 teaspoon Korean red chile flakes
1 teaspoon toasted sesame seeds
1 teaspoon sugar

First!

Blot the tofu with paper towels so it won't splatter as much when you fry it.

Tofu is made by boiling then pressing soy milk. It's been part of Korean cuisine for more than a thousand years.

Cut the tofu block in half, then into 1/2-inch slices.

Heat a nonstick pan with olive oil over medium heat and place the tofu in the pan, without overlapping.

Put the lid on the pan and cook for about 5 minutes.

You'll hear the tofu sizzle and pop. Flip the tofu and close the lid again. Leave the tofu for about 5 to 10 minutes, until both sides are . . .

Crispy & golden Brown!

Let's Make the Sauce

Thinly slice the green onion.

In a bowl, mix the green onion, soy sauce, vinegar, chile flakes, sesame seeds, and sugar.

Now

Place the tofu on a serving plate and pour the sauce over the top.

You can also serve the sauce on the side.

ENJOY

Spicy Bok Choy

(Cheonggyeongchae Muchim)

Traditionally this recipe is made with various wild mountain vegetables like ferns, balloon flower roots, and water dropworts. But this time, I've used bok choy, a leafy Chinese green, because it's versatile and easier to find in the United States. You can also use broccoli rabe or Swiss chard.

Cooking time: 20 minutes   Makes 2 cups

INGREDIENTS

4 large bok choy
Salt
2 tablespoons gochujang
  (red chile paste)
1 tablespoon sugar
1 tablespoon soy sauce
1 tablespoon rice vinegar
1 tablespoon toasted sesame oil
1 teaspoon toasted sesame seeds
1 teaspoon Korean red chile flakes
1 clove garlic, minced
Pine nuts, for garnish

Break off the leaves from the heads of bok choy and wash the leaves in cold water.

TAK!

Add a pinch of salt to a big pot of water and heat to a boil.

Blanch the bok choy for about 3 minutes.

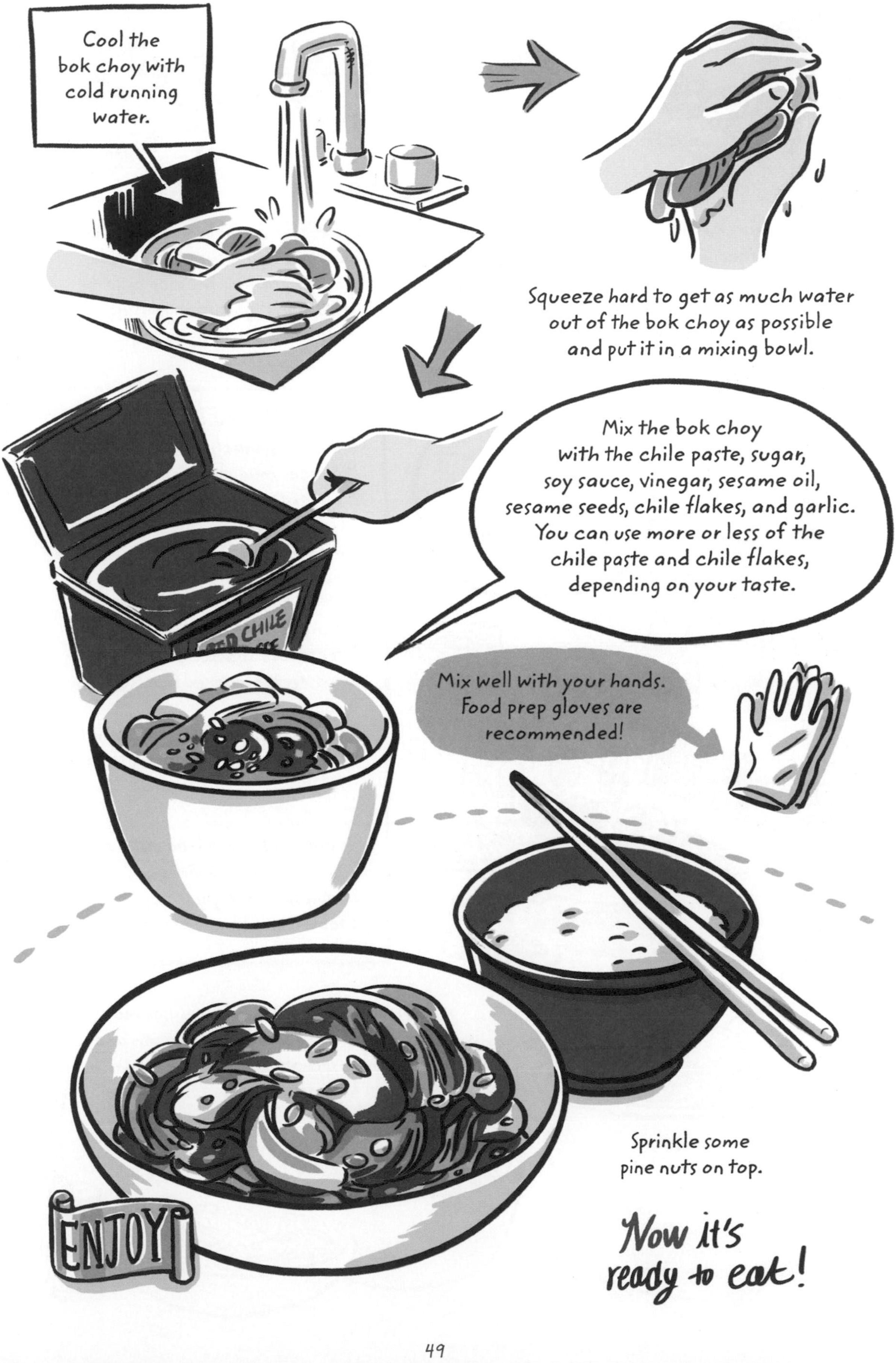
Cool the bok choy with cold running water.
Squeeze hard to get as much water out of the bok choy as possible and put it in a mixing bowl.
Mix the bok choy with the chile paste, sugar, soy sauce, vinegar, sesame oil, sesame seeds, chile flakes, and garlic. You can use more or less of the chile paste and chile flakes, depending on your taste.
Mix well with your hands. Food prep gloves are recommended!
Sprinkle some pine nuts on top.
ENJOY
Now it's ready to eat!

Mixed Veggies & Rice in a STONE BOWL

(Dolsot Bibimbap)

Dolsot means "stone pot," bibimbap means "mixed rice": dolsot bibimbap is usually cooked with rice topped with various blanched vegetables and served with a side of spicy sauce. You can add galbi, bulgogi or tofu for more protein. The rice absorbs the yummy flavors of all of the different ingredients, and it gets crispy sitting in the bottom of the stone bowl as you eat—my favorite part of this dish.

Cooking time: 1 hour Makes 4 servings

This is a pretty simple dish to make—most of the work goes into prepping the toppings. First, wash all the vegetables.

INGREDIENTS

8 ounces spinach
8 ounces mung bean sprouts
8 ounces gosari (boiled fern)*
  (see next page)
1 medium zucchini
8 ounces shiitake mushrooms
Salt
1 teaspoon soy sauce
4 teaspoons toasted sesame oil
2 cups freshly cooked rice (see page 18)
4 eggs
Toasted sesame seeds, for garnish
Toasted seaweed, crushed, for garnish

- - - - - - - - - - - - - - - - - -

Spicy Sauce
1/3 cup gochujang (red chile paste)
3 tablespoons rice vinegar
2 tablespoons sugar
1 tablespoon toasted sesame oil

Add a pinch of salt to a big pot of boiling water and blanch the spinach and mung bean sprouts separately, then cool them with cold running water.

Drain and gently squeeze out as much water as you can and season the spinach and mung bean sprouts separately, each with 1/2 teaspoon salt and 1 teaspoon toasted sesame oil.

MUNG BEAN SPROUTS

SESAME OIL

Cut the zucchini in half lengthwise and then into ¼-inch slices. Remove the stems from the shiitake mushrooms and cut them into thin slices too.

Sauté the zucchini and shiitake mushrooms separately with salt and a dash of sesame oil, and set it aside.

생고사리
NET 1½
BOILED FERN

Gosari* are the stems of young brake ferns. You can find them in the refrigerated section of Korean grocery stores, cleaned, boiled, and packaged in water.

Drain the gosari and cut them into pieces about 2 inches long. Sauté for a couple of minutes with 1 teaspoon of sesame oil and 1 teaspoon of soy sauce. Set aside.

Heat up four ttukbaegi (Korean earthenware pot; for an alternative use cocottes) over high heat each with ½ tablespoon water and 1 teaspoon sesame oil. Add 1 cup of cooked rice and arrange the cooked vegetables on top per serving. Put on the lid and cook for a minute. When you hear the rice pop, lower the heat to medium and cook for 4 more minutes.

To make the spicy sauce, mix the chile paste, vinegar, sugar, and sesame oil.

Fry the eggs sunny-side up with runny yolks and serve one atop each serving of dolsot bibimbap and sprinkle with toasted sesame seeds and crushed toasted seaweed for garnish.

Serve the spicy sauce on the side and add the sauce according to your taste. Mix everything together!

ENJOY

Dotorimuk is my mom's favorite side dish.

Can you bring one more? You know this isn't enough for me!

Sure.

Her fifth serving of dotorimuk.

But she never makes it at home. She only eats it at restaurants.

One day at the Korean grocery market I spotted...

acorn starch for 30 cents?!

SALE

Most Koreans love dotorimuk but I've never seen anyone making it at home. Everyone just buys it premade. How does one make the dotorimuk?

05 28 20

Direction
2 cups acorn starch
5 cups water
½ t salt
½ t cooking oil
Heat the water with acorn starch, cooking oil and salt and make a firm paste for 20 minutes on the medium heat. chill in the r...

Heat the water with acorn starch and boil then chill it in the refrigerator? It sounds so simple that I think I can make this. And good, it hasn't expired yet.

Making the acorn starch from scratch would be a pain in the butt. But since you can just buy it, I wonder why no one makes dotorimuk at home.

I could make a refrigerator full of dotorimuk with just one package!

Five minutes into cooking.

CLUMP

Strange. It's already hardening so fast. But the package said to heat it for 20 minutes over medium heat.

Ten minutes into cooking.

HUFF HUFF

I've even turned the heat down to the lowest but it's still hardening too fast! This can't be right... or maybe this is why no one makes it at home?

I've cooked it for exactly 20 minutes and...

ROCK SOLID

SHAKE!

it's completely stuck to the bottom of the pot. I can't even pour it into the baking pan!

Oh, what's that? Alien rocks?

Hey, Dengki! How do I fix this?

Dunno. Who makes dotorimuk at home these days?

Hmm. When in doubt, ask the Internet. Wow, all of these recipes online use half as much starch than what I've just used!

On the second try...

Are you making dotorimuk?

Yup. 1 cup acorn starch to 5 cups water. That's more like it!

swoosh~

Don't be afraid to fail on the first try! Sometimes even the package directions are not perfect. Try a few recipes to find the one you like!

NOT ONLY for the SQUIRRELS!
Acorn Jelly SALAD
(Dotorimuk)

Acorn jelly is a unique food that's found only in Korean cuisine. The jelly doesn't have much taste other than a hint of woodsy tannin but it is an excellent base that can carry other flavors. It's gluten-free, vegan, and low in calories.

Cooking time: 15 minutes Resting time: 1 day Makes 6 cups

A long time ago, Koreans gathered acorns in the woods, peeled them, milled them, soaked them in water, and dried them all by hand to make acorn flour. It was hard, tedious, and time-consuming work. Hardly anyone makes it from scratch these days. Now you can buy the acorn flour at Korean grocery stores.

Mi...

MINE!

INGREDIENTS

5 cups water
1 cup acorn starch
1 teaspoon olive oil
4 tablespoons soy sauce
2 tablespoons toasted sesame oil
1 tablespoon Korean red chile flakes
2 teaspoons sugar
2 cups baby lettuce
1 small Kirby cucumber, julienned
1/2 small carrot, julienned
2 green onions, white and green parts, thinly sliced on the diagonal
2 teaspoon toasted sesame seeds

In a pot over high heat, heat the water with acorn starch and oil and whisk well. When it starts to boil, turn down the heat to medium and stir well for about 10 minutes, until it thickens.

In a mixing bowl, combine the soy sauce, sesame oil, red chile flakes and sugar, then toss in the baby lettuce, cucumber, carrot, and green onions and mix well. Lay the acorn jelly rectangles in a serving dish and pour the veggie mixture over the top. Lastly, sprinkle the toasted sesame seeds on top. It's ready to eat!

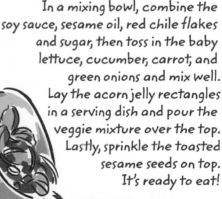

3"
7"
7"

Pour it into a 7-inch square pan, cover with plastic wrap and chill it in the refrigerator overnight; then cut it into about 1/2-inch-thick, 2-inch-wide rectangles.

TOASTED SESAME SEEDS

ENJOY!

Chapter 3
Meat and Poultry

INTRO TO KOREAN BARBECUE

There are three things that make Korean barbecue special.

The marinade,

the grill,

and ssam (lettuce and perilla wrap).

The MARINADE

The main ingredients in the marinade for Korean barbecue are: Soy sauce, sugar, garlic, and ginger.

Fruits such as Asian pear, kiwi, or apple are also used to add a natural sweetness. They also make the meat juicy and tender at any doneness.

People sometimes use soda instead.

Some cuts of meat, like pork belly (samgyupsal), are served without being seasoned or marinated.

It's much thicker than bacon.

The GRILL

Korean barbecue restaurants have a charcoal grill or gas burner in the middle of the table so you can grill throughout your meal and enjoy hot off the grill.

The direct source of high heat chars the meat quickly and seals in the juice. The excess fat drips away and makes the meat leaner.

chrr...

Sitting around a fire and grilling meat together is probably the oldest form of dining in human history.

Those distant memories of happy dinner must still reside in us, which may be why Korean barbecue is so enjoyable for everyone. There are some outdoor barbecue joints in Korea that use a slab of heated stone for a grill!

SSAM means wrap in Korean. Korean barbecue comes with an assortment of sides to make your own wraps. Ssam makes the meal more flavorful and nutritious.

The dipping sauce (ssamjang) is usually made with soybean paste, sesame oil, garlic, green onion, sesame seeds, and Korean red chile paste (gochujang).

You can find perilla leaves at Korean grocery stores during the summer. Korean perilla leaves have a hint of refreshing pinelike aroma that cuts through the fattiness of the meat.

When you order the pork belly barbecue, the dipping sauce is toasted sesame oil mixed with salt and freshly ground pepper.

HOW TO MAKE A SSAM

First, lay a lettuce or perilla leaf (or both!) in your hand.

Put a spoonful of rice in the middle.

DUNK!

Dip the meat in the dipping sauce and put it on top of the rice.

AHH~

Wrap everything into a ball and pop it into your mouth!

If you want an extra kick, add green onion salad (page 57) and slices of garlic and chile pepper to your ssam.

You can also grill garlic, onion, mushrooms, and kimchi and put it in your wrap.

The trick is not to pile on too much in the ssam. The wrap should be a manageable one-bite size.

You sure you can put all that in your mouth?

NO PROBLEM!

WOW. Expandable jaw!?

JUST GRILL IT!

You can easily make authentic Korean barbecue at home. All you need is one of these two handy devices to grill the meat of your choice on your dining table just like at Korean restaurants.

All Korean families own a portable gas burner or electric grill pan. You can find them at most Korean grocery stores and also in many American department stores.

Electric grill pan

Portable gas burner

Large tongs and a pair of kitchen shears are useful for handling the sizzling meat.

Quick Side Dish Recipe
GREEN-ONION-SALAD
(Pajeori)

The thinner the better!

Pajeori is a staple side dish served with Korean barbecue. Its garlicky, oniony flavor cuts through the greasiness of the meat. Make it just before grilling the meat because it wilts fast.

Cut four large green onions in half lengthwise and then cut them into thin, 5-inch strips.

Soak the green onions in ice water for 10 minutes, then drain. This gets rid of the sliminess of the green onions and makes them crunchier.

Toss the drained green onions with 2 teaspoons rice vinegar, 2 teaspoons toasted sesame oil, 1 teaspoon sugar, 1 teaspoon Korean red chile flakes, and 1 teaspoon fish sauce. Now, it's done!

ENJOY

GRILLED BEEF SHORT RIBS
(Galbi)

Galbi means ribs, and it is generally made with beef short ribs, though it can also be made with chicken or pork. It is very easy to make at home. I marinate a large batch and freeze single portions in resealable plastic bags so I can defrost and grill delicious beef whenever I want to.

Marinating time: 3 hours   Prep time: 10 minutes   Makes 4 to 6 servings

There are two different cuts of galbi you can find at Korean grocery stores.

L.A. galbi is cut vertically and has several thin pieces of bones in a row.

Regular galbi is cut horizontally, with a thick slab of meat attached to one big bone.

INGREDIENTS

3 pounds beef short ribs
1/2 small kiwi
1 small yellow onion
6 cloves garlic
1 (1-inch) piece fresh ginger
1/2 cup soy sauce
3 tablespoons soju (Korean rice liquor)
1 tablespoon toasted sesame oil
1 tablespoon granulated sugar
2 tablespoons brown sugar
1 teaspoon freshly ground black pepper
3 green onions, white and green parts

- - - - - - - - - - - - - - - - - - - -

Dipping Sauce (Ssamjang)
2 tablespoons soybean paste
1 tablespoon gochujang (red chile paste)
1 tablespoon toasted sesame oil
1 green onion, white and green parts, thinly sliced
1 teaspoon toasted sesame seeds
1 clove garlic

First, soak the ribs in plenty of cold water for 30 minutes to drain out the liquid.

The water will turn pink.

Then blot the ribs with paper towels to remove excess water.

There are many variations of galbi marinade. Some people use fruit juices, honey, corn syrup, or sodas like Coke or Sprite to sweeten and tenderize the meat. I use kiwi in my recipe, but the most traditional versions use Asian pears.

Let's make the Marinade

Peel the kiwi, yellow onion, garlic, and ginger. Chop them into chunky pieces and blend them in a food processor with the soy sauce, soju, sesame oil, granulated sugar, brown sugar and pepper.

wee

Slice the green onions thinly and mix them into the marinade.

Put a layer of beef in a rectangular container and cover it with a generous amount of marinade. Repeat until there's no more beef and marinade left. Cover the container with a lid or plastic wrap and refrigerate for 3 hours. Then it's ready for grilling!

Use kitchen shears to cut the galbi into bite-size pieces as you grill it!

For the dipping sauce (ssamjang), mix the soybean paste, chile paste, sesame oil, green onion, sesame seeds, and garlic.

Chrr..

ENJOY

Cook the meat on high heat and then turn and keep the heat at a low setting when the meat is cooked through, so that it is kept warm throughout your meal.

SOY GARLIC BEEF
OVER RICE
(Bulgogi Dupbap)

Bulgogi means fire meat. Thinly sliced beef chuck steak is most often used in this dish, but you can also use chicken or pork. Traditionally, Asian pear is used in the marinade to make the meat tender and sweet. I've substituted kiwi, which is easier to find at most grocery stores and also tenderizes the meat more quickly than Asian pear.

Prep time: 10 minutes Marinating time: 3 hours Makes 4 servings

You can find thinly sliced beef for bulgogi at Korean grocery stores. These are much thinner than regular steaks and are cut into $^1/_8$-inch slices.

First, blot the beef dry with paper towels.

INGREDIENTS

$1^1/_2$ pounds round eye beef chuck, bulgogi cut
1 medium yellow onion
8 cloves garlic
1 ($^1/_2$-inch) piece fresh ginger
$^1/_2$ small kiwi
5 tablespoons soy sauce
2 tablespoons soju (Korean rice liquor)
2 tablespoons toasted sesame oil
$2^1/_2$ tablespoons sugar
$^1/_2$ teaspoon freshly ground black pepper
4 green onions, white and green parts, plus thinly sliced green onions, for garnish
5 shiitake mushrooms
4 cups freshly cooked rice (page 18)
Toasted sesame seeds, for garnish

Let's make the marinade!

Peel the yellow onion, garlic, ginger, and kiwi. Chop the kiwi and half of the onion into chunky pieces. Blend the chopped onion and kiwi with the garlic, ginger, soju, soy sauce, sugar, 1 tablespoon of the sesame oil, and the pepper.

Put a layer of beef in a rectangular container and cover it with a generous amount of marinade. Repeat until there's no more beef and marinade left. Cover the container with a lid or plastic wrap and refrigerate for for 3 hours.

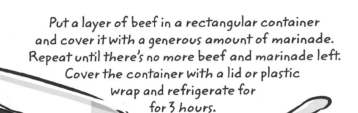

3 HOURS LATER

Cut the remaining half of the onion into thin slices, and cut the green onions into 3-inch pieces. Wash and discard the stems of the shiitake mushrooms and cut them into thin slices.

Heat a pan over high heat with 1 tablespoon of sesame oil and sauté the beef for a minute, then add the yellow onion, green onion, and shiitake mushrooms and sauté for a few more minutes, until all the ingredients are cooked.

So ♥ easy

Serve it over freshly cooked rice and sprinkle toasted sesame seeds and thinly sliced green onions on top for garnish!

ENJOY

BRAISED BEEF in SOY SAUCE

(Jangjorim) with eggs!

Just a little bit of this salty beef goes a long way! This was my favorite lunch box dish during my Korean school days. You can add as many hard-boiled eggs as you want. Jjangjorim can be stored up to 2 weeks in the refrigerator.

Cooking time: 45 minutes Makes 4 cups

You can use any cut of lean beef including round eye, steak, brisket, or chuck. Cut the meat into 2- to 3-inch cubes.

INGREDIENTS

$1\frac{1}{2}$ pounds lean beef, cut into cubes
8 cups water
1 large yellow onion, peeled and left whole
1 (4-inch-square) dashima (dried kelp) (page 14)
4 dried shiitake mushrooms
10 dried anchovies
1 tablespoon peppercorns
6 hard-boiled eggs
5 cloves garlic, peeled
1 cup soy sauce
1 tablespoon sugar
1 red or green chile, sliced on the diagonal (optional)

The water will turn pink.

Soak the cubes in plenty of cold water for 15 minutes to drain out the liquid.

Meanwhile, bring the water to a boil with the onion, dashima, dried shiitake mushrooms, dried anchovies, and peppercorns.

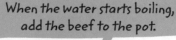

When the water starts boiling, add the beef to the pot.

Boil over high heat for 15 to 20 minutes, until the beef is well cooked.

With a slotted spoon, remove the beef, dashima, and shiitake mushrooms and set the broth aside. Strain and discard the peppercorns and onion. Strain the broth again through cheesecloth or a coffee filter. Measure 1 cup of broth and set aside. This broth is great for soups and stews, so save the remaining broth for another use!

When the dashima and shiitake mushrooms are cool enough to handle, cut them into thin strips.

The straining process gets rid of excess fat so it doesn't form a layer of hardened fat on top when it's chilled.

Shred the beef into small, bite-size strips with your hands, following the grain of the meat.

Everything goes into the Pot!

Add the sliced chile if you want it spicy!

Finally ♡

Pack everything, including the cooking liquid in a container and chill it in the refrigerator.

Slice the eggs into bite-size pieces just before serving. Serve cold.

Peel the eggs and put them in a pot with the shredded beef, dashima, mushrooms, garlic cloves, the 1 cup broth, the sugar, and the soy sauce. Boil for 10 minutes over medium heat.

ENJOY

SPICY PORK OVER RICE
(Jeyuk Dupbap)

Dupbap means over rice and there are many variations of this recipe. You can also switch out the pork for beef or chicken. The tender, juicy meat in the rich, spicy sauce is simply irresistible.

Cooking time: 30 minutes Makes 4 servings

First, CHOP EVERYTHING!

Let's cut all of the vegetables. Cut the carrots into thin slices.

INGREDIENTS

1 medium carrot
8 ounces green cabbage
1 large yellow onion
5 green onions, white and green parts
1 green chile pepper
6 cloves garlic, peeled
1 (1/2-inch) piece fresh ginger, peeled
1 pound pork shoulder, thinly sliced*
   (see next page)
1 tablespoon olive oil
2 tablespoons soju (Korean rice liquor)
1 tablespoon sugar
1 tablespoon Korean red chile flakes
3 tablespoons soy sauce
3 tablespoons gochujang (red chile paste)
4 cups freshly cooked rice (page 18)
Toasted sesame oil, for garnish
Toasted sesame seeds, for garnish

Quarter and core the cabbage. Then cut it into 1-inch-wide, 2-inch-long strips.

CHOP! CHOP!

Chop the onion into big bite-size pieces; cut 3 of the green onions into 3-inch pieces and thinly slice the remaining 2 green onions for garnish; and thinly slice the chile into rings. Mince the garlic and ginger.

Slice the pork into 2-inch strips.

*Choose a cut of pork that has nice thin marbling all over, rather than thick, chunky lines of fat.

Heat up a wok with the oil over high heat and stir-fry the pork with the garlic, ginger, soju, sugar, chile flakes, and 1 tablespoon of the soy sauce for about 5 minutes, until the pink hue of the pork is gone.

RED CHILE PASTE

Then add the carrot, cabbage, onion, and green chile to the wok and mix in the chile paste and the remaining 2 tablespoons of soy sauce.

Stir-fry over medium heat for 5 to 10 minutes, until all of the vegetables are cooked.

The LAST STEP

Add the green onions and cook for a minute or two more.

Put the freshly cooked rice on a serving dish and pour the pork stir-fry on top. Drizzle with sesame oil and sprinkle with sesame seeds and thinly sliced green onions for garnish.

ENJOY

BOILED PORK BELLY WRAP
(Bossam)

Bossam means wrap. This dish originated from the meals served during kimjang, the collective kimchi-making event (see page 23). People would wrap the pork with freshly salted napa cabbage, saeujeot (tiny salted shrimp), and radish slaws, which are the main ingredients in kimchi. Bossam is often a part of festive meals in Korea.

Cooking time: 50 minutes Makes 6 servings

For the wrap, look for a good-quality napa cabbage with fresh, not-too-thick leaves. Cut off the bottom end of the napa cabbage and separate the leaves. Cut the big outer leaves in half lengthwise. Rinse them in cold running water, then drain.

Sprinkle the salt and pour the water all over the leaves. Set aside for 40 minutes. Toss once in a while for even salting.

INGREDIENTS

2 leeks
1 medium yellow onion
10 cloves garlic
1 ($1\frac{1}{2}$-inch) piece fresh ginger
3 pounds pork belly
2 teaspoons peppercorns
3 dried Korean red chile peppers
4 tablespoons soju (Korean rice liquor)
4 tablespoons soybean paste
3 tablespoons soy sauce
2 tablespoons honey

- - - - - - - - - - - - - - -

Napa Cabbage Wrap
2 pounds napa cabbage
$3\frac{1}{2}$ tablespoons kosher salt
4 cups water

- - - - - - - - - - - - - - -

Radish Slaw
$1\frac{1}{2}$ pounds daikon radish, cut into thin matchsticks
$\frac{1}{3}$ cup Korean red chile flakes
3 green onions, white and green parts, thinly sliced
6 cloves garlic, minced
3 tablespoons fish sauce
2 tablespoons sugar
$\frac{1}{2}$ tablespoon saeujeot (tiny salted shrimp)

After cutting the roots off, rinse the leeks thoroughly to get all of the dirt out, then cut each into 2 or 3 chunky logs. Peel the onion, garlic, and ginger.

✧ SO PERFECT! ✧

Rinse the pork belly in cold running water and pat it dry with paper towels.

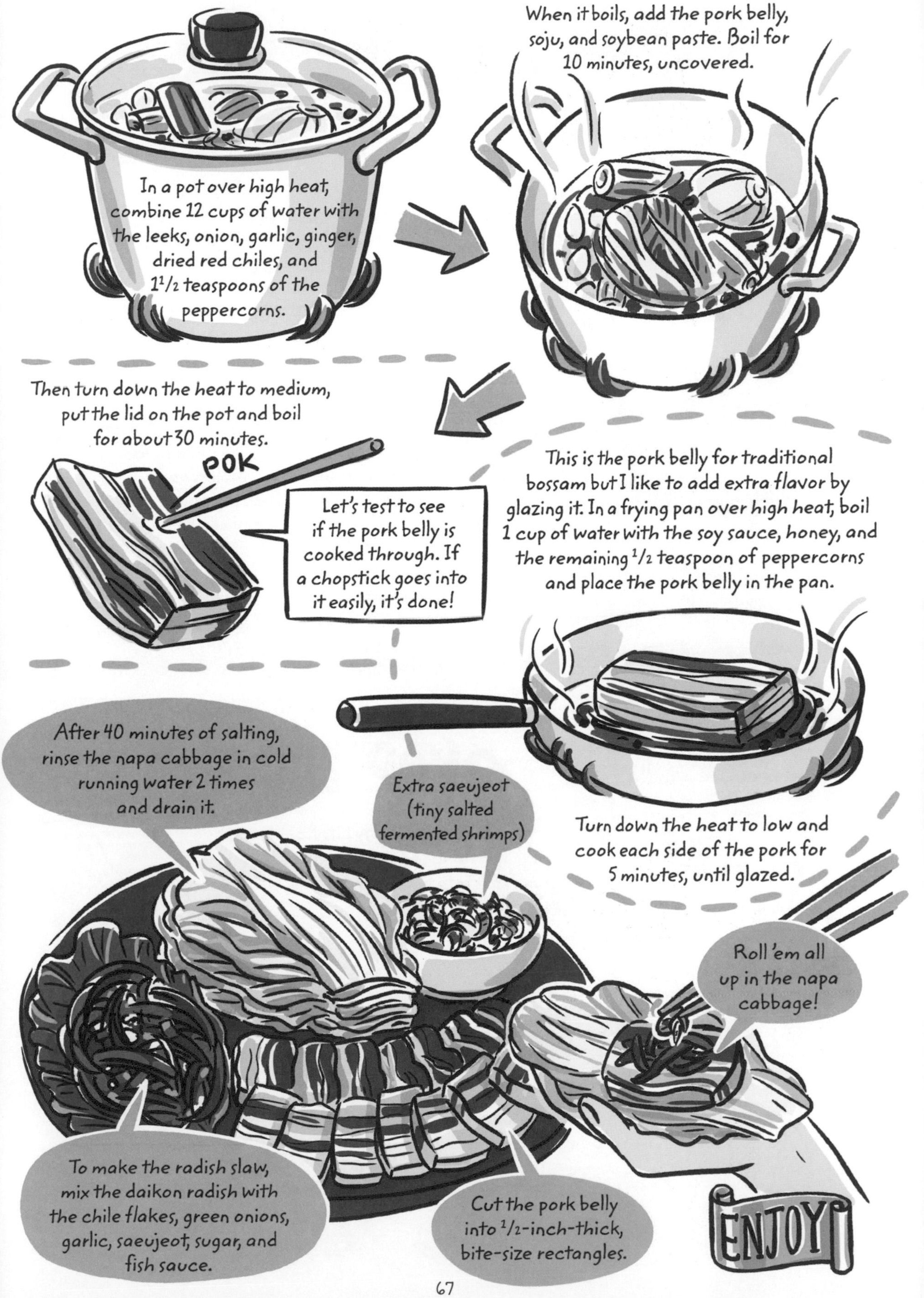
In a pot over high heat, combine 12 cups of water with the leeks, onion, garlic, ginger, dried red chiles, and 1 1/2 teaspoons of the peppercorns.
When it boils, add the pork belly, soju, and soybean paste. Boil for 10 minutes, uncovered.
Then turn down the heat to medium, put the lid on the pot and boil for about 30 minutes.
POK
Let's test to see if the pork belly is cooked through. If a chopstick goes into it easily, it's done!
This is the pork belly for traditional bossam but I like to add extra flavor by glazing it. In a frying pan over high heat, boil 1 cup of water with the soy sauce, honey, and the remaining 1/2 teaspoon of peppercorns and place the pork belly in the pan.
Turn down the heat to low and cook each side of the pork for 5 minutes, until glazed.
After 40 minutes of salting, rinse the napa cabbage in cold running water 2 times and drain it.
Extra saeujeot (tiny salted fermented shrimps)
Roll 'em all up in the napa cabbage!
To make the radish slaw, mix the daikon radish with the chile flakes, green onions, garlic, saeujeot, sugar, and fish sauce.
Cut the pork belly into 1/2-inch-thick, bite-size rectangles.
ENJOY

HOT! CHiLe CHiCKeN STeW
(Dakbokkeumtang)

This is my favorite chicken dish because of its bold flavor. It's also easy to make and quite a crowd pleaser. My mom used to make it for my birthday when I was young.

Cooking time: 45 minutes   Makes 4 to 6 servings

RED CHILE PASTE

INGREDIENTS

2 pounds boneless, skinless chicken thighs
10 cloves garlic, peeled
2 large yellow onions
1 (1/2-inch) piece fresh ginger, peeled
1 large carrot
2 large yellow potatoes
1/2 cup gochujang (red chile paste)
2 tablespoons soy sauce
2 tablespoons soju (Korean rice liquor)

2 tablespoons toasted sesame oil
1 tablespoon Korean red chile flakes
1 tablespoon sugar
1 1/2 cups water
4 green onions, white and green parts, plus thinly sliced green onion for garnish
1 Korean green chile (optional)

Gochujang (Korean red chile paste) is the major ingredient in this dish; it is also used in many other Korean dishes. If you don't have it in your pantry already, it's time for you to go on an adventure to the Korean supermarket!

prep the meat

Trim the fatty bits from the chicken thighs and cut them into big bite-size cubes.

...& the Veggies!

There's no such thing as too much garlic in Korean cooking. Mince all of the garlic cloves!

Cut the yellow onions into big bite-size chunks.

And mince the ginger.

Wash and peel the carrot and the potatoes. Then cut them into 1-inch cubes.

Now, let's marinate the meat.

Mix the chicken with the garlic, onion, ginger, red chile paste, soy sauce, soju, sesame oil, chile flakes, and sugar in a pot.

Set the pot over high heat and cook the marinated meat mixture for about 5 minutes, then add the potatoes, carrot, and water. Cover, turn down the heat to medium, and boil for about 25 minutes.

More Heat

Meanwhile, chop 4 of the green onions into 2-inch pieces and the green chile into chunky diagonal rings. Add the green onions and chile to the pot for the last 5 minutes of cooking. (You can leave out the green chile if you want it less spicy.)

Stir occasionally so everything gets evenly cooked.

Add a bit of thinly sliced green onion on top for color just before serving.

Let's eat!

ENJOY

69

GINSENG CHICKEN SOUP
(Samgyetang)

In Korea, this chicken soup is traditionally eaten on the hottest days of the summer to restore your energy. The delicate herby aroma of ginseng mellows out the gamy smell of chicken and gives the soup a clean, savory flavor. You can find a young whole chicken (weighing 2 pounds or less) at Korean grocery stores.

Prep time: 1 hour Cooking time: 1 hour 30 minutes Makes 4 servings

Ginseng is a Korean root vegetable that is highly valued for its medicinal properties. You can find it at Korean grocery stores.

Because of its shape, ginseng is called insam in Korean, which means "the human root."

Ginseng roots vary in size.

INGREDIENTS

1½ cups sweet rice
8 dried red dates (jujubes)
5 cloves garlic
8 chestnuts
2 ounces ginseng
1 (2-pound) young chicken
Salt and pepper

- - - - - - - - - -

Bonus Porridge
Toasted sesame oil
1 green onion, white and green parts, thinly sliced diagonally.

Let's PREP the INGREDIENTS!

First, soak the sweet rice in plenty of water for an hour.

Tips:

Here's the easy way to peel the chestnuts.

OW!

With a sharp knife, score each chestnut with an "X," then wash them to give them a little moisture.

Microwave them for a minute.

CUT
OUT THEN ROLL

Remove the pits from the dried dates and roll the flesh of the dates. Peel the garlic and chestnuts. Wash the ginseng and cut it into 2-inch pieces.

Use a towel— the chestnut is very hot!

Crack open the chestnuts and peel off the shells, leaving the golden nut inside.

70

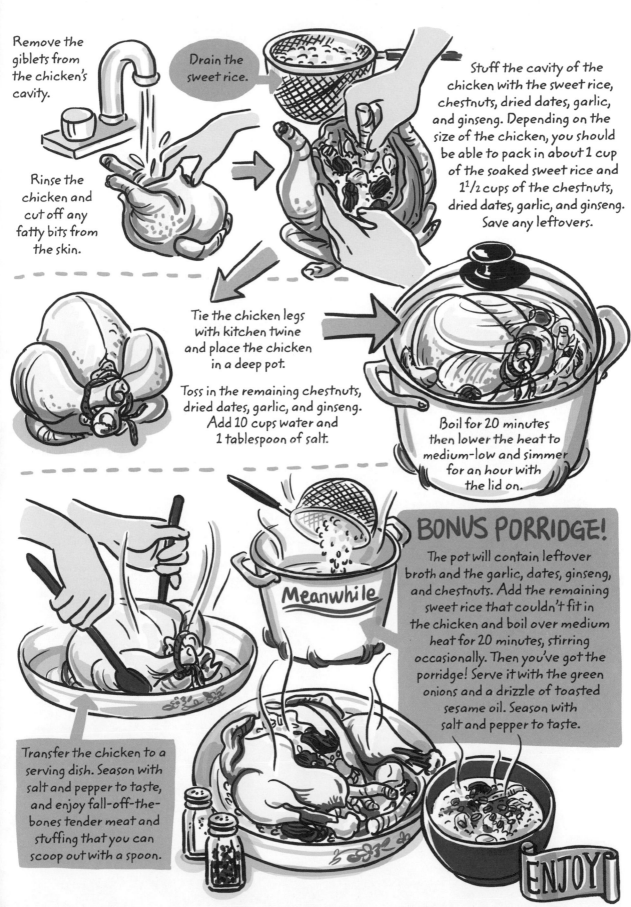

Remove the giblets from the chicken's cavity.

Rinse the chicken and cut off any fatty bits from the skin.

Drain the sweet rice.

Stuff the cavity of the chicken with the sweet rice, chestnuts, dried dates, garlic, and ginseng. Depending on the size of the chicken, you should be able to pack in about 1 cup of the soaked sweet rice and $1^1/_2$ cups of the chestnuts, dried dates, garlic, and ginseng. Save any leftovers.

Tie the chicken legs with kitchen twine and place the chicken in a deep pot.

Toss in the remaining chestnuts, dried dates, garlic, and ginseng. Add 10 cups water and 1 tablespoon of salt.

Boil for 20 minutes then lower the heat to medium-low and simmer for an hour with the lid on.

Meanwhile

BONUS PORRIDGE!

The pot will contain leftover broth and the garlic, dates, ginseng, and chestnuts. Add the remaining sweet rice that couldn't fit in the chicken and boil over medium heat for 20 minutes, stirring occasionally. Then you've got the porridge! Serve it with the green onions and a drizzle of toasted sesame oil. Season with salt and pepper to taste.

Transfer the chicken to a serving dish. Season with salt and pepper to taste, and enjoy fall-off-the-bones tender meat and stuffing that you can scoop out with a spoon.

ENJOY!

Chapter 4
Seafood

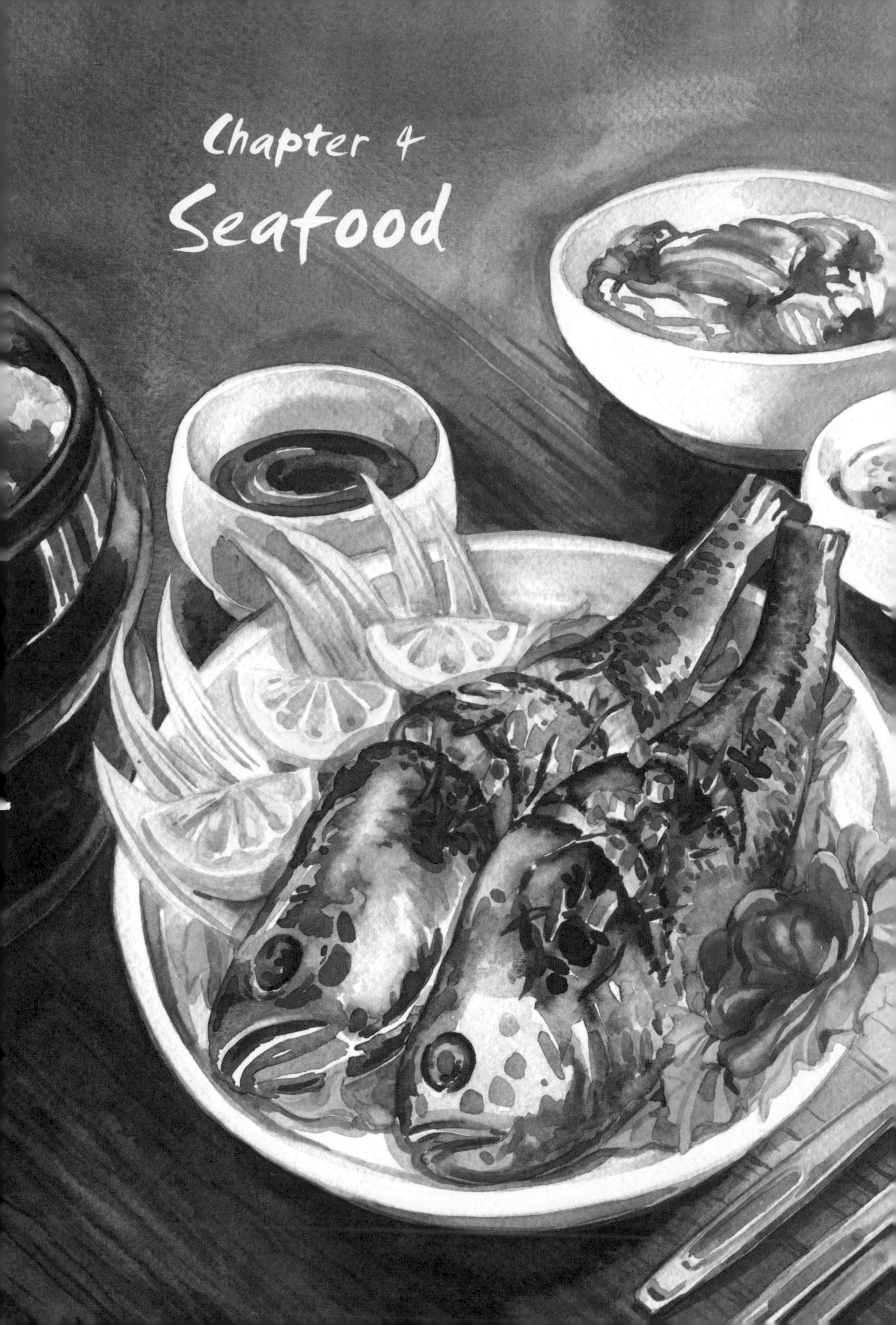

INTRO TO KOREAN SEAFOOD

Baby octopus

Spoon worm

Sea cucumber

Squid

Sea urchin

Crab

Sea squirt

Abalone

Korea is surrounded by three seas and we eat all kinds of seafood in every way possible. Seafood markets in Korea are full of weird creatures that can be eaten raw, straight out of the tank.

Some of these are so fresh that they continue to fight for their lives even in your mouth.

The octopus is stuck on my gums!

Yikes! It's still moving!

WIGGLE

WIGGLE

WIGGLE

Koreans also enjoy seafood in the most rotten state.

Phew, it stinks so much, I can't even open my eyes. But it tastes heavenly!

Hongeo is skate that has fermented in its own uric acid.

Cured seafood, called jeotgal, is common in Korea.

Cured pollock intestines

Cured oysters

Cured fish roe

Cured squid

Cured anchovies

Cured crabs

They are my favorite side dishes.

We also air-dry all kinds of seafood to preserve it.

Shrimp

File fish

Pollock

Anchovy

Cuttlefish

Kelp

These are eaten as snacks or in wraps or made into side dishes or soups.

RUN!

There's really nothing Koreans won't eat!

Thinly sliced jellyfish is blanched then tossed in vinegar and sugar and served as a salad.

Hidden seafood: Even if you can't see it, you are most likely eating seafood in every Korean meal because saeujeot (tiny salted fermented shrimp) and fish sauce are ubiquitous in Korean cuisine.

SPICY OCTOPUS
→ OVER RICE ←
(Nakji Dupbap)

This is a supersimple, delicious seafood dish to soak up your rice with. I've used frozen octopus in this recipe to cut down the prep time. You can also use squid instead of the octopus.

Cooking time: 20 minutes Makes 3 or 4 servings

DISCARD

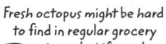

Fresh octopus might be hard to find in regular grocery stores, but if you do find it, make sure you get rid of the intestine and clean it before using it.

You can find already cleaned and cut octopus in the frozen seafood section of Korean grocery stores.

FROZEN
Octopus
Keep Frozen
낙지볶음
2 lbs

INGREDIENTS

2 pounds octopus, cleaned
  and cut into bite-size pieces
1 medium carrot, peeled
1 Korean green or red chile pepper
1 medium onion
3 green onions, white and green parts
1/4 medium green cabbage
3 cloves garlic, peeled
1 (1/2-inch) piece fresh ginger, peeled
2 tablespoons gochujang
  (red chile paste)
2 tablespoons Korean red chile flakes
1 tablespoon soy sauce
2 teaspoons sugar
3 tablespoons olive oil
Salt
1 tablespoon toasted sesame oil
4 cups freshly cooked rice
  (page 18)
Toasted sesame seeds, for garnish

Prep the Veggies!

Wash all of the veggies. Cut the carrot and chile into thin pieces and cut the onion, green onions, and cabbage into chunky bite-size pieces.

The SAUCE

Mix the chile paste, 1 tablespoon of the chile flakes, soy sauce, and sugar. Set aside.

Slice the ginger, then crush the garlic and ginger.

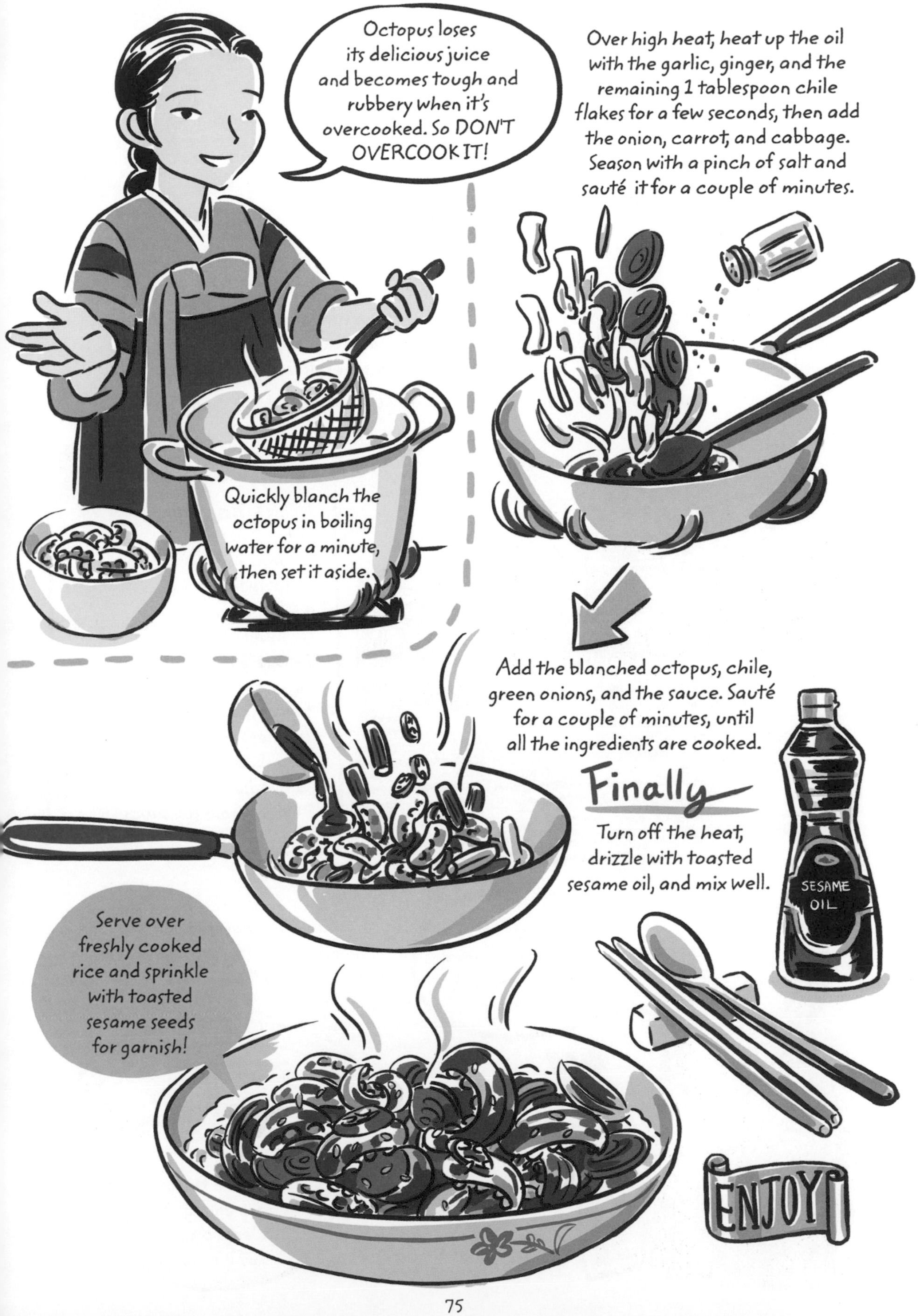
Octopus loses its delicious juice and becomes tough and rubbery when it's overcooked. So DON'T OVERCOOK IT!
Quickly blanch the octopus in boiling water for a minute, then set it aside.
Over high heat, heat up the oil with the garlic, ginger, and the remaining 1 tablespoon chile flakes for a few seconds, then add the onion, carrot, and cabbage. Season with a pinch of salt and sauté it for a couple of minutes.
Add the blanched octopus, chile, green onions, and the sauce. Sauté for a couple of minutes, until all the ingredients are cooked.
Finally
Turn off the heat, drizzle with toasted sesame oil, and mix well.
SESAME OIL
Serve over freshly cooked rice and sprinkle with toasted sesame seeds for garnish!
ENJOY

Tangy Seaweed SALAD
(Miyeok Naengchae)

This is my all-time favorite side dish. Miyeok (dried seaweed) may be a bizarre, never-before-seen ingredient to some Westerners, but it's been part of Asian cuisines for centuries. It has a silky, flexible and slightly meaty texture that is different from leafy greens grown on land. It's full of vitamins and minerals and also low in calories.

Prep time: 40 minutes Cooking time: 10 minutes Makes 5 cups

INGREDIENTS

1 ounce miyeok (dried seaweed)
1 Kirby cucumber
1/2 small carrot, peeled
1 clove garlic
1/2 small yellow onion
3 tablespoons rice vinegar
2 tablespoons sugar
2 teaspoons Korean red chile flakes
2 tablespoons soy sauce

Break off about an ounce of dried seaweed from the package.

Soak the seaweed in a deep mixing bowl full of cold water for 40 minutes.

Make sure the bowl is deep enough for at least 8 cups of water.

Meanwhile... let's prep the Veggies!

How to julienne cut cucumber and carrot.

First, thinly slice the cucumber on the diagonal.

Stack up a few slices together and cut them into matchsticks. Slice and cut the carrot into matchsticks, too.

Mince the garlic clove. Thinly slice half an onion. The thinner the slices, the better!

40 minutes Later...

You will notice the seaweed has expanded to almost 10 times its volume— back to its original form. Drain the soaking water and rinse the seaweed in cold water 2 times.

Squeeze out as much water as possible.

Then chop the seaweed into 2-inch strips.

Chill it in the refrigerator before serving!

Mix the seaweed with the onion, carrot, cucumber, garlic, rice vinegar, sugar, chile flakes, and soy sauce.

ENJOY!

BRAISED DAIKON with SAURY
(Mu Kkongchi Jorim)

Saury is a small, oily fish that tastes so similar to mackerel that it is sometimes called mackerel pike. This dish is a good example of how Koreans use seafood in everyday meals: it's easy and inexpensive and the leftovers taste good.

Cooking time: 40 minutes   Makes: 4 to 6 servings

INGREDIENTS

$1\frac{1}{2}$ pounds daikon radish

1 large yellow onion

3 green onions, white and green parts

6 cloves garlic

1 ($\frac{1}{2}$-inch) piece fresh ginger, peeled

1 Korean green chile pepper (optional)

1 (14-ounce) can saury

$\frac{1}{3}$ cup soy sauce

2 tablespoons Korean red chile flakes

2 teaspoons sugar

$\frac{2}{3}$ cup water

Optional

Daikon radish is one of the most beloved vegetables in Korea. Fresh daikon has a spicy kick and a crunchy texture, but when it is cooked, it becomes sweet and soft.

First!

Rinse the daikon radish in cold water.

Then lightly peel the outer layer and cut it into 1-inch-thick, chunky pieces.

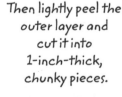

Chop the onion into chunky bite-size pieces and the green onions into 3-inch pieces. Mince the garlic and ginger.

If you want it extra spicy, cut the green chile pepper into chunky rings.

Lay the radish evenly in the bottom of a pot and put the onion (not the green onions) on top. Then pour in the can of saury with its liquid.

PACIFIC SAURY

Let's make the Sauce.

In a small bowl, mix the soy sauce, chile flakes, sugar, garlic, and ginger and pour it on top of everything in the pot along with the water.

Boil over high heat for about 10 minutes, then cover and lower the heat to medium for about 15 minutes. Gently stir occasionally so the flavors meld.

The Last Touch

Add the green onions and the green chile, if using, and boil for another 3 minutes.

Now, it's ready to eat!

ENJOY!

Shishito Peppers with Dried Anchovies & Fish Cakes

(Kkwarigochujjim)

Shishito peppers have a wrinkly delicate skin that absorbs flavors very well. They are usually sweeter than regular chile peppers, but they can sometimes be surprisingly spicy. I recommend you taste one before cooking.

Cooking time: 20 minutes Makes 4 cups

Eomuk (fish cake) is made with ground white fish and flour. Think of it as fish sausage. It comes in various shapes and sizes. You can find it in the frozen section of Korean or Japanese grocery stores.

INGREDIENTS

$1\frac{1}{4}$ pounds shishito peppers
5 sheets fish cake
$\frac{1}{2}$ small yellow onion
4 cloves garlic, peeled
2 tablespoons olive oil
1 cup small dried anchovies
6 tablespoons soy sauce
2 tablespoons sugar
1 tablespoon toasted sesame oil
Toasted sesame seeds, for garnish

WE ARE ALL EOMUK!

In this recipe, we are using the flat kind.

Make sure you get the small anchovies, not the big ones, for making the broth.

About 1-inch-long or less.

They are so small that you don't have to remove their heads or guts.

Prep the Shishito Peppers

Break off and discard the stems and wash the peppers in cold water.

Tok!

Then poke a few holes in the peppers with a toothpick.

OUCH!

Cut the fish cakes into about 1-inch, bite-size strips.

Slice the onions into half-moons and mince the garlic.

Heat up a large wok with oil over high heat and sauté the onion, dried anchovies and fish cake with 2 tablespoons of the soy sauce and 5 tablespoons of water for about 5 to 10 minutes, until the fish cake softens and the onion is translucent.

charr...

Then add the shishito peppers with the remaining 4 tablespoons of soy sauce, the sugar, 1 tablespoon of water, and the garlic. Stir well over medium heat for about 10 minutes.

THE LAST TOUCH~

Turn off the heat, drizzle with the toasted sesame oil, and sprinkle with some toasted sesame seeds.

If you can't find shishito peppers at your grocery store, you can still use this recipe to make eomuk bokkeum (sautéed fish cake) by adding more fish cakes and onion instead of the shishito peppers.

ENJOY

SO FRESH! RAW FISH, SALAD BOWL
(Hoedupbap)

This dish is full of fresh veggies and fish and packed with vitamins and proteins. It's one of the healthiest, tastiest and easiest dishes in Korean cuisine. Its tangy, spicy dressing is the key to tying all of the ingredients together.

Cooking time: 10 minutes Makes 2 servings

You can use any kinds of sushi-grade fish in this dish. The most commonly used are salmon, tuna, snapper, and flounder.

You can find sushi-grade fish and fish roe in the refrigerated seafood section of Korean and Japanese grocery stores.

INGREDIENTS

1 Kirby cucumber
$1/2$ small carrot, peeled
2 green onions, white and green parts
4 large Romaine lettuce leaves
8 ounces sushi-grade salmon, tuna, snapper or flounder
$1/4$ small Asian pear, peeled
1 clove garlic, peeled
Juice of $1/2$ lemon
$1/4$ cup gochujang (red chile paste)
3 tablespoons soy sauce
2 tablespoons rice vinegar
1 tablespoon sugar
2 teaspoons toasted sesame seeds, plus more for garnish
2 cups freshly cooked rice (page 18)
1 ounce tobiko (flying fish roe)
Toasted seaweed, crushed, for garnish

Tobiko is the tiny roe of flying fish. It comes in plastic packs or small glass jars.

It's usually dyed bright orange, red, or green.

wee···!

CUT THE Veggies...

Slice the cucumber and carrot into thin matchsticks.

Slice the green onions into thin rings.

ROLL 'EM

DISCARD

Cut off the thick, white bottoms from the lettuce leaves. Roll the leaves into a cigar shape and slice into thin ribbons.

...& the fish~!

Find the grain of the fish, then slice against the grain into 1/4-inch strips. Cut the strips into bite-size pieces.

Against the grain

← GRAIN →

Cutting against the grain makes the fish more tender.

The DRESSING ♡

In a blender, combine the Asian pear with the garlic, lemon juice, chile paste, soy sauce, vinegar, and sugar and blend into a smooth paste.

Fruits add natural sweet and tangy flavors to the dressing and also make it light and refreshing.

SOY SAUCE

RED CH PAST

RIC VINE

SUGAR

MIX EVERYTHING!

Add the green onions and 2 teaspoons of the sesame seeds into the dressing and mix well. Serve the dressing on the side and mix it into the salad to your taste.

Put the freshly cooked rice in the bottom of each bowl and cover it with lettuce. Arrange the fish, cucumber, carrot, and tobiko on top.

Sprinkle with crushed seaweed and toasted sesame seeds.

ENJOY!

PAN-FRIED YELLOW CROAKER

(Jogi Gui)

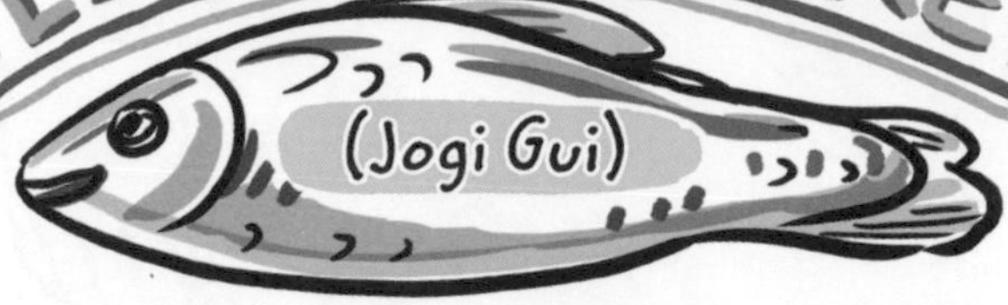

Because of its great taste, yellow croaker is called jogi in Korean, which means boosting energy. You can use this recipe to cook other small oily fish such as pike, or fillet of mackerel or belt fish.

Cooking time: 15 minutes Serves 2 people

INGREDIENTS

2 small yellow croakers, (each about 8 inches long)
1 tablespoon sweet rice flour
1 tablespoon corn starch
Salt
1 tablespoon olive oil
2 tablespoons soy sauce
2 tablespoons rice vinegar
Pickled ginger, for serving
Slices of lemon, for serving

PREP THE FISH!

Run the knife against the scales to remove them on both sides of the fish.

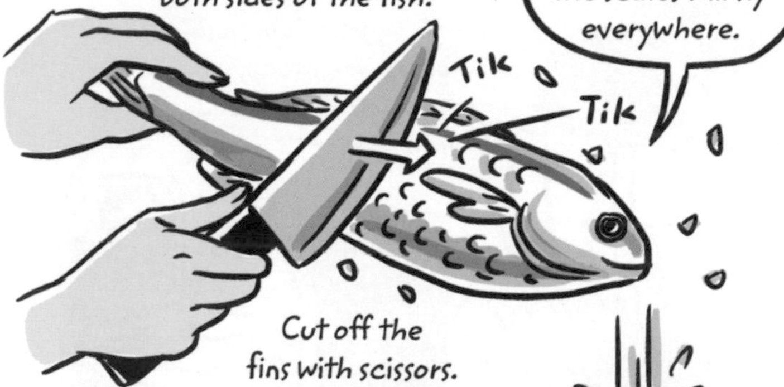
Do this in the sink; otherwise the scales will fly everywhere.
Tik
Tik

Cut off the fins with scissors.

Rinse the fish in cold running water, including inside the gills. Rinse any scaly residue off the knife.

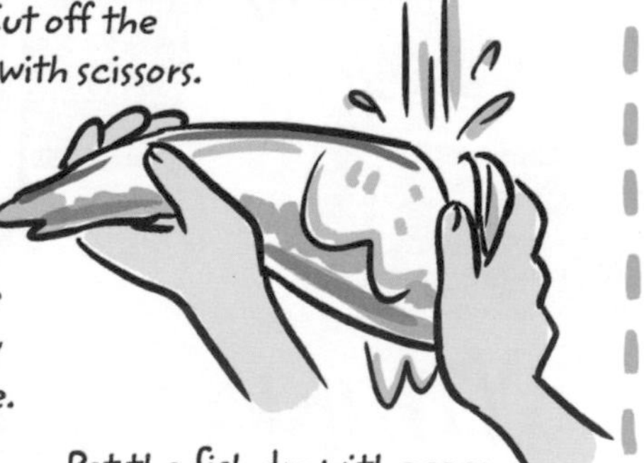

Mix the sweet rice flour and cornstarch together on your countertop.

Pat the fish dry with paper towels and, with a knife, make a couple of slits on the body. Sprinkle a pinch of salt and rub the sweet rice flour and cornstarch on both sides.

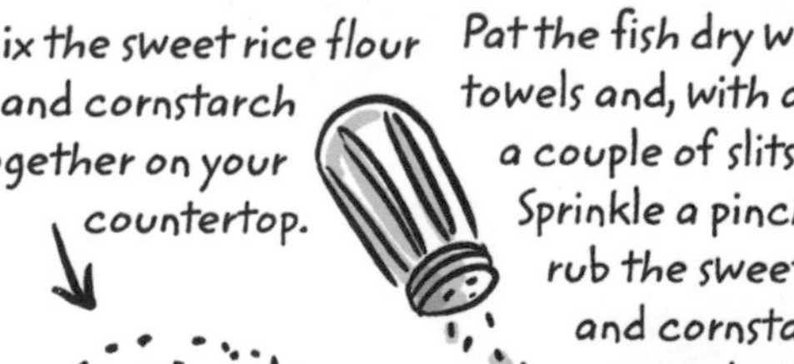

Heat up a pan with oil over high heat.

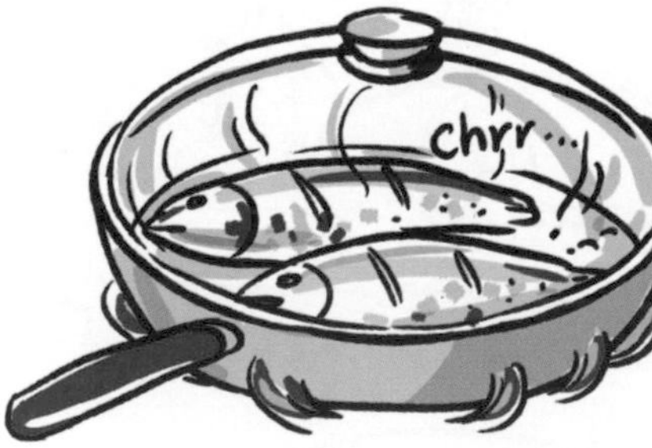
Chrr...

Place the fish in the pan and cover. Sear the skin for a few seconds, then reduce the heat to medium-low. Cook for about 3 to 5 minutes, flip and cook the other side. Cook until the flesh turns solid white and is no longer translucent.

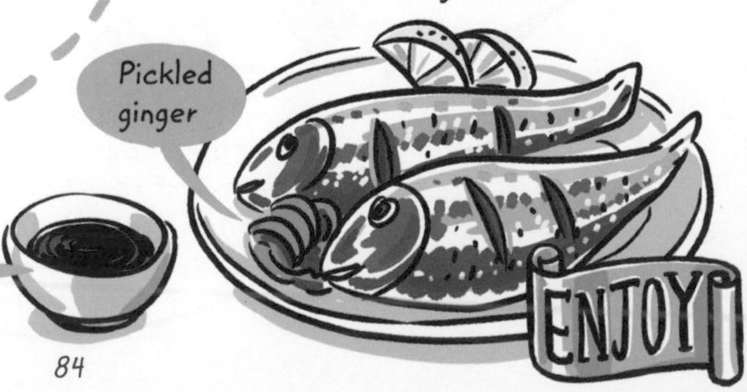
Pickled ginger
ENJOY

Mix the soy sauce and vinegar to make the dipping sauce.

The Legend of Gulbi

Gulbi is salted and air-dried yellow croaker. Yeonggwang, a fishing town on the southwestern shore of Korea, is famous for making the best gulbi.

Twelfth-century Kaesong, the capital of Goryeo. Goryeo was the kingdom that preceded Chosen which would become modern Korea.

Your majesty, all I did was for you and your kingdom! I am your loyal servant!

Lee Jagyeom was a powerful politician and a man of pride. He was accused of treason and banished to Yeonggwang.

At Yeonggwang, Lee tasted salty dried yellow croaker for the first time.

This humble fish is the local speciality, m'lord.

What a remarkable taste and texture! His Majesty would love this fish.

The Korean alphabet had yet to be invented. Noble Koreans wrote in Chinese characters back then.

Deliver this box of fish to His Majesty. This is just a gift; I'm not asking for a pardon.

This banishment won't make me bend my will. I am not sorry for what I did!

The Chinese characters he wrote mean "not to bend my will," which is pronounced "gulbi" in Korean.

Kaesong, King's palace.

This is the best fish I've ever had! What is it called, gulbi?

I want gulbi at every meal from now on.

Lee died in exile and the salty dried yellow croaker from Yeonggwang was named gulbi after his letter. Since then, gulbi has become the most sought-after and highly prized fish throughout Korea. But this is just a legend.

The true origin of the word gulbi comes from its curved shape, which is formed by tying it with a rope for air-drying.

The curved shape is called "gubi" in Korean; it became "gulbi" later on.

Chapter 5
Soups and Stews

FIRE & ICE

Intro to the Extreme Temperatures in Korean Dining

Ttukbaegi (earthenware pot)

Cast-iron serving dish for stir-fries

Koreans love piping hot food so much that often Korean stews are served in an earthenware pot (ttukbaegi) to keep it hot for a long time. They are sometimes even placed on a portable burner to keep it bubbling throughout the meal.

Koreans lovingly describe the sensation of piping hot spicy broth burning through our guts as . . .

TOO HOT!!

AH~♥ SIWONHADA!

. . . which means "how cool" (as in temperature). We use the same expression to describe totally opposite sensations, such as in drinking cold water or jumping into a pool. Weird, isn't it?

When Koreans eat cold noodles and cold kimchi soups, we like to add ice chunks to the bowl to keep the food extra cold.

Nothing is too hot or too cold for Korean soups. We like it as long as it's not lukewarm.

In Korean slang, we say "eyeol chiyeol," which means "fire to fire." If a force is acting upon us, we deal with it by using the same force, instead of running away.

Ah~ siwonhada!

Ah~ siwonhada!

Hence, it's the Korean tradition to eat piping hot ginseng chicken soup on the hottest day in the summer and ice-cold radish soups in the winter.

SOFT ♥ TOFU SOUP

(Sundubu Jjigae)

This stew is traditionally served piping hot in a small earthenware vessel called a ttukbaegi. You can add all kinds of ingredients to this stew along with the soft tofu, such as seafood, beef, pork, and kimchi, depending on your taste!

Cooking time: 40 minutes   Makes 2 servings

If you're using fresh clams, soak them in cold water with plenty of salt for 3 hours to get all the sand out. If you're using frozen clams, you can skip this step.

As salty as the ocean.

INGREDIENTS

8 ounces fresh or frozen littleneck clams
10 large dried anchovies
3 cups water
1/2 small zucchini
6 cloves garlic, peeled
1/2 small yellow onion
3 spring onions, white and green parts
1 (3 1/2-ounce) package fresh enoki mushrooms
1 tablespoon cooking oil
4 ounces pork, any cut; diced small
1 teaspoon soju (Korean rice liquor)
4 teaspoons fish sauce
1 cup frozen seafood mix
3 tablespoons Korean red chile flakes
2 (11-ounce) packages soft tofu
1 Korean green chile (optional)
1 egg
Toasted sesame oil, for drizzling

Let's make the broth.

Discard the heads and the black guts of the dried anchovies and put them in a strainer ball.

DISCARD

In a small pot, boil the water with the dried anchovies for 20 minutes.

Meanwhile...

Wash the zucchini and cut it into bite-size cubes. Mince the garlic.

Chop the onion into small bite-size pieces.

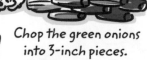

Chop the green onions into 3-inch pieces.

Cut off the roots of the enoki mushrooms and discard. Rinse them clean.

In a ttukbaegi or other small pot, drizzle in the oil and cook the pork with garlic, onion (not the green onion), soju, and 1 teaspoon of the fish sauce for about 3 minutes.

Char....

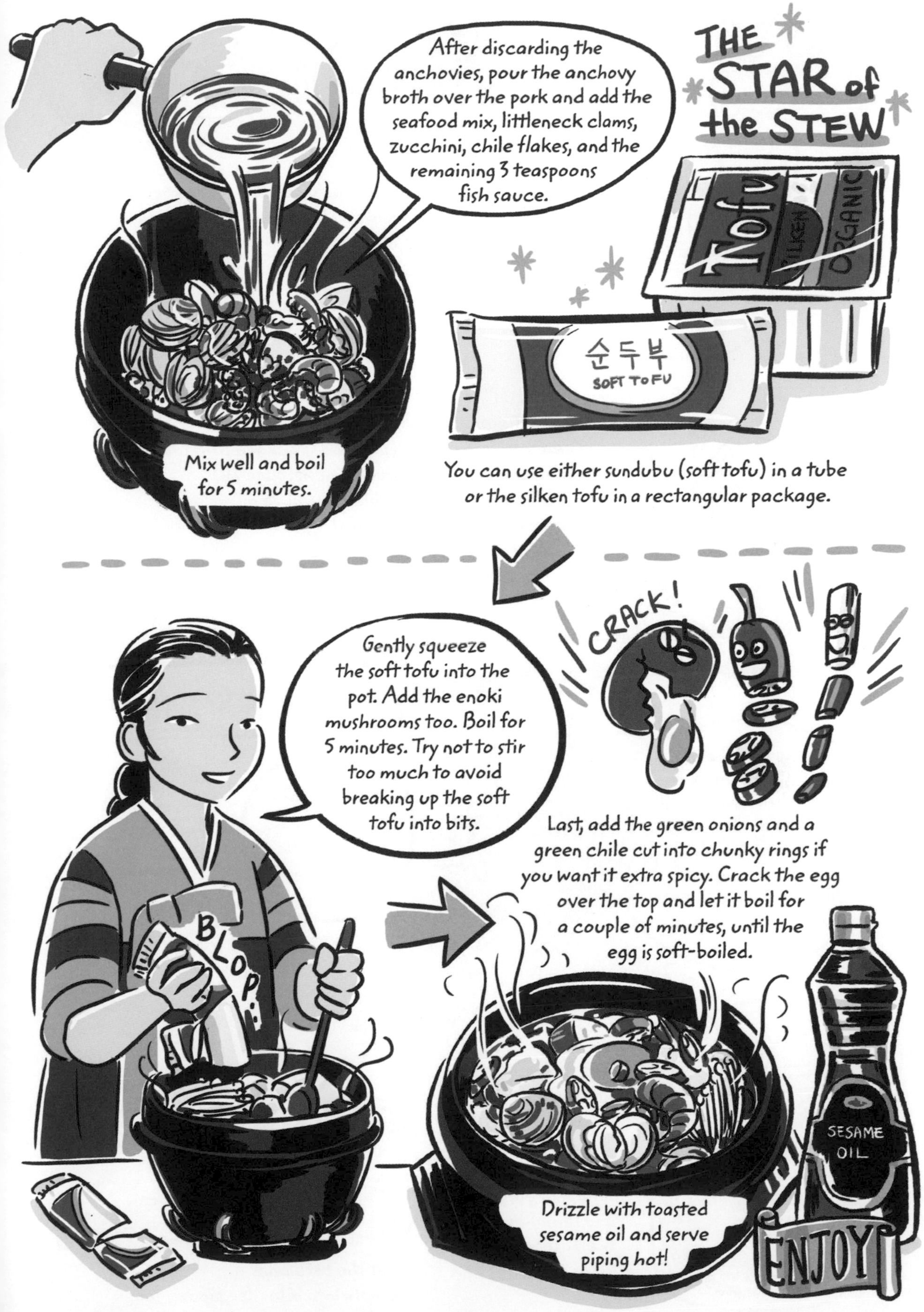
After discarding the anchovies, pour the anchovy broth over the pork and add the seafood mix, littleneck clams, zucchini, chile flakes, and the remaining 3 teaspoons fish sauce.
Mix well and boil for 5 minutes.
THE STAR of the STEW
Tofu
SILKEN
ORGANIC
순두부
SOFT TOFU
You can use either sundubu (soft tofu) in a tube or the silken tofu in a rectangular package.
Gently squeeze the soft tofu into the pot. Add the enoki mushrooms too. Boil for 5 minutes. Try not to stir too much to avoid breaking up the soft tofu into bits.
BLOP.
CRACK!
Last, add the green onions and a green chile cut into chunky rings if you want it extra spicy. Crack the egg over the top and let it boil for a couple of minutes, until the egg is soft-boiled.
SESAME OIL
Drizzle with toasted sesame oil and serve piping hot!
ENJOY

Ahh... It makes you warm inside!

Kimchi Stew
(Kimchi Jjigae)

SPICY!

This simple and hearty recipe is the easiest way to use up old kimchi. Jjigae means stew in Korean, and it basically consists of throwing everything in a pot with a bit of water and boiling it. It's so easy!

Cooking time: 40 minutes   Makes 4 servings

Pork belly is the #1 selling pork cut in Korea. It's easy to find in Asian grocery stores, but it might not be available at typical American grocery stores.

INGREDIENTS

8 ounces pork belly
1 (1-pound) package firm tofu
3 cups kimchi (page 26)
1 tablespoon olive oil
1 cup water
1/2 cup kimchi juice
1 tablespoon Korean red chile flakes
2 teaspoons sugar
1 Korean green chile (optional)

Can't find the pork belly in the store? No worries. Just use Spam! It's a common ingredient in Korean comfort food—we consume the most Spam in the world after Guam and Hawaii!

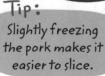

SPAM

First, CHOP CHOP!

Remove the skin from the pork belly and slice it into bite-size pieces.

Tip: Slightly freezing the pork makes it easier to slice.

SKIN

Like wine and cheese, kimchi becomes more flavorful as it ages. Kimchi that has been aged for several months is called mukeunji and it makes the best base for stews.

The smellier the better!

Cut the tofu and kimchi into bite-size pieces, too.

Heat a pot with the oil over high heat and stir-fry the pork with the kimchi for about 5 minutes. Then add the water, kimchi juice, chile flakes, and sugar to the pot and mix well. Cover, turn down the heat to medium, and boil for about 15 minutes.

Charr.. Chirr..

It smells so delicious!

Final Step...

Add the tofu and the sliced green chile, if you want it extra spicy, and boil for another 10 minutes.

NOW it's ready to be served.

Best Served Piping Hot!

It might be quite spicy, so serving it with a glass of water would be wise.

ENJOY

91

SOYBEAN PASTE SOUP with CLAMS

(Jogye Doenjangguk)

Cooking time: 40 minutes   Makes 4 to 6 servings

Doenjangguk means soybean paste soup and it's the second most missed food for expatriate Koreans after Kimchi Jjigae (see page 90). Miso, the Japanese soybean paste, tastes a little milder and sweeter than doenjang, the Korean soybean paste. You can use either in this recipe, depending on your taste.

INGREDIENTS

1 pound fresh or frozen littleneck clams
1 king oyster mushroom
1 small yellow onion
3 cloves garlic, peeled
2 medium potatoes
1 medium zucchini
1 tablespoon cooking oil
2 tablespoons fish sauce
4 cups water
3 tablespoons soybean paste
3 green onions, white and green parts
1/2 (1-pound) package firm tofu
1 Korean green chile pepper (optional)

If you're using fresh clams, submerge them in cold water with a handful of salt for 3 hours, then rinse them clean with cold running water before cooking.

Salt water causes the clams to spit out sand and grit.

You can use either fresh or frozen littleneck clams. If they're frozen, defrost them by placing them in a sink with cool running water.

Clean the king oyster mushroom with a damp paper towel. Cut and discard all of the root part (see page 112). Dice the mushroom and onion into small bite-size pieces. Mince the garlic.

Wash and peel the potatoes and cut them into 1-inch cubes. Wash the zucchini and cut into 1-inch cubes too.

Let's heat things up!

Heat up a pot with the cooking oil over high heat and sauté the clams with the yellow onion, garlic, oyster mushroom, and fish sauce for about 5 minutes. Add the potatoes, water, and soybean paste and mix well. Put the lid on and boil for about 10 minutes.

Yumm~
It smells so good! Add the zucchini to the pot, cover and boil for 10 more minutes.

Meanwhile...
Cut the green onions into 2-inch-long pieces and the tofu into bite-size pieces. If you want some spicy kick, cut the green chile into chunky rings.

Add the tofu, green onion, and green chile to the pot and boil for a couple of minutes.

Now it's ready to eat!

ENJOY

93

SEAWEED SOUP WITH BEEF

(Sogogi Miyeokguk)

This soup is so nutritious that Korean women eat it to regain their strength after giving birth. It is also the Korean tradition to eat this soup on birthdays, as a reminder of your mother's hard labor. But you can enjoy it on your unbirthdays too!

Soaking time: 30 minutes Cooking time: 40 minutes Makes 4 to 6 servings

Before cooking...

Soak the miyeok in a large bowl of water for about 30 minutes.

Add at least 8 cups of cold water

The miyeok will expand and become soft and silky.

Drain the miyeok.

INGREDIENTS

1 ounce miyeok (dried seaweed)
8 ounces lean beef (chuck shoulder, sirloin steak, or round eye)
6 cloves garlic, peeled
1 tablespoon olive oil
1 tablespoon soju (Korean rice liquor)
2 tablespoons gukganjang (light soy sauce)
Toasted sesame oil, for drizzling

Cut the miyeok into 4-inch strips.

Cut the beef into small bite-size cubes and mince the garlic.

Heat up a big pot with the oil over high heat and sauté the beef with the garlic, soju, and 1 tablespoon of the soy sauce for about 5 minutes.

Add the miyeok and the remaining 1 tablespoon of soy sauce to the pot and sauté for a couple of minutes to allow the miyeok to soak up the beef flavor.

Then add 8 cups of water and boil over medium heat for 20 minutes.

Drizzle a bit of toasted sesame oil on top, and now it's ready to serve!

You can also make this soup vegan by making the broth with 4 ounces of shiitake mushrooms and 1/4 cup soybean paste instead of the beef!

ENJOY

SOYBEAN SPROUT SOUP

(Kongnamulguk)

SO REFRESHING!

This light and refreshing soup is part of a common breakfast in Korea, served in its own bowl next to a bowl of rice. The soybean sprout is full of nutrition and fiber, and this soup will get you back to feeling hydrated and clear-headed in no time.

Cooking time: 35 minutes   Makes: 4 to 6 servings

INGREDIENTS

1 pound soybean sprouts
3 green onions, white and
   green parts
1/2 small yellow onion
2 cloves garlic, peeled
10 large dried anchovies
6 cups water
3 tablespoons gukganjang
   (light soy sauce)
2 teaspoons Korean red
   chile flakes
1 teaspoon sugar
1 (4-inch-square) dashima
   (dried kelp)
Toasted sesame oil, for drizzling

First, Place the sprouts in a pot and rinse them in cold water 2 or 3 times.

If there are any brown spots on the sprouts, discard them.

Drain the cleaned sprouts and set aside.

Cut 2 of the green onions into 2-inch pieces and thinly slice the rest for the garnish.

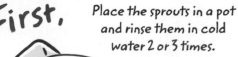

Cut the yellow onion into bite-size pieces. Mince the garlic.

The anchovy broth is probably the most used broth in Korean cooking because it's inexpensive and easy to make. All you need are some dried anchovies and dried kelp (dashima).

Dried anchovies come in various sizes. Use the big ones to make the broth.

Break off the heads and discard the black guts, which taste bitter.

Then put the anchovies inside a large strainer ball and lock it. If you don't have a strainer ball, no big deal. You'll just have to fish 'em out by hand later.

DRIED ANCHOVIES

DISCARD

To the pot of soybean sprouts, add the water, garlic, onion (not the green onions), soy sauce, chile flakes, sugar, and dried kelp. Put the strainer ball with the dried anchovies in the pot and close the lid. Boil over medium heat for 15 minutes.

Drizzle with toasted sesame oil and sprinkle sliced green onions on top before serving!

Add the 2-inch pieces of green onions and boil for a minute. Turn off the heat and discard the kelp and anchovies.

SESAME OIL

ENJOY

BEEF & DAIKON
— SOUP —
(Sogogimuguk)

Mu~?

The Korean word for radish is "mu" and guess what? Beef and daikon radish make a great soup together! This simple soup, served with a bowl of barley rice, will warm you right up.

Cooking time: 45 minutes Makes 4 to 6 servings

~ CHOPPING TIME ~

Wash the daikon radish and lightly peel the outer layer.

Then cut it into about 1-inch squares that are 1/8-inch thick.

Slice the green onions into 1-inch pieces. Mince the garlic.

Cut the beef into bite-size chunks.

Let's make the Soup!

A dash of soju gets rid of the gamy smell of the meat.

Heat up a big pot with oil over high heat and sauté the beef with garlic, 1 tablespoon of the soy sauce and the soju. Cook for about 5 minutes, until the beef is no longer red.

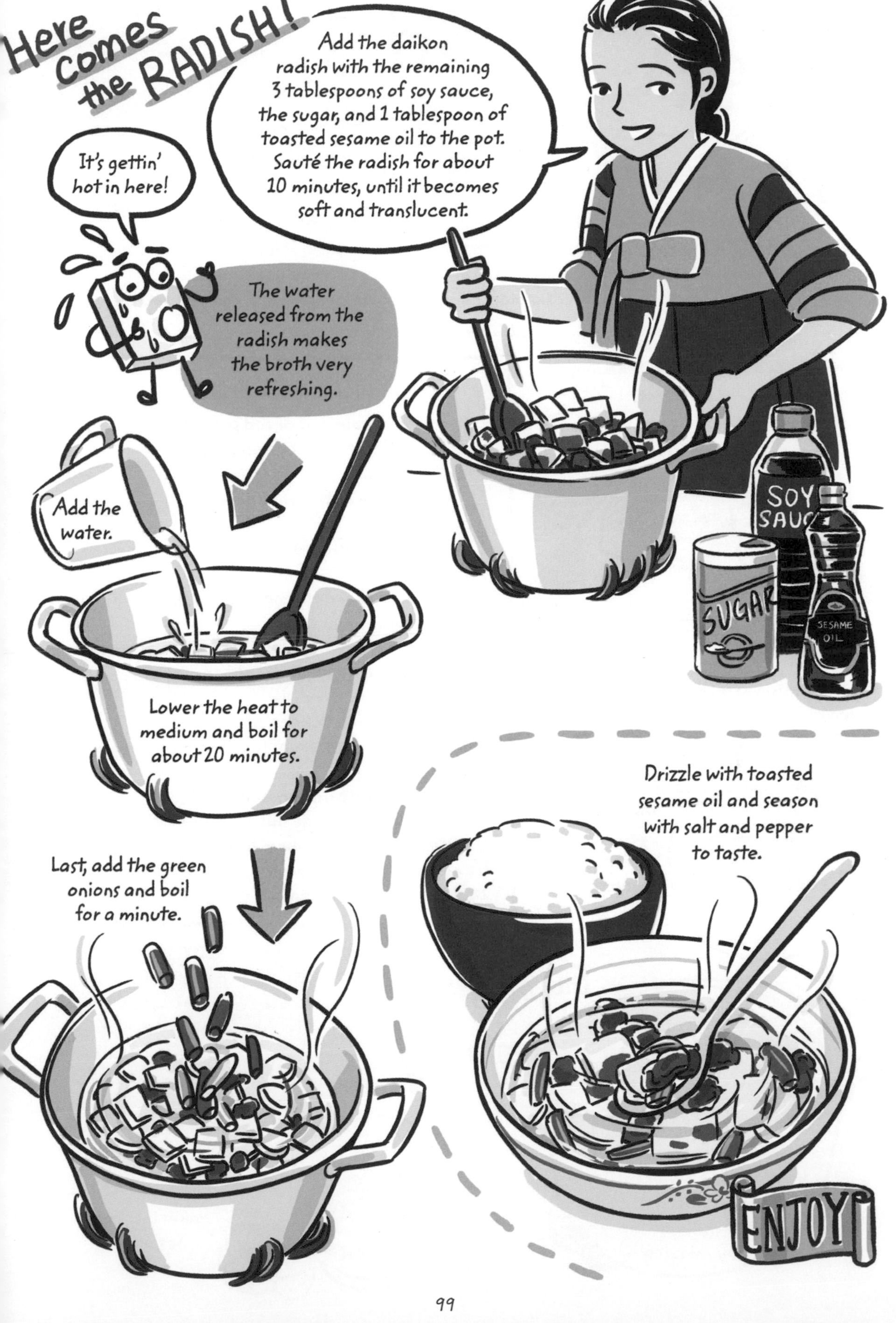
Here comes the RADISH!
Add the daikon radish with the remaining 3 tablespoons of soy sauce, the sugar, and 1 tablespoon of toasted sesame oil to the pot. Sauté the radish for about 10 minutes, until it becomes soft and translucent.
It's gettin' hot in here!
The water released from the radish makes the broth very refreshing.
Add the water.
SOY SAUC
SUGAR
SESAME OIL
Lower the heat to medium and boil for about 20 minutes.
Drizzle with toasted sesame oil and season with salt and pepper to taste.
Last, add the green onions and boil for a minute.
ENJOY

SPICY FISH STEW

(Maeuntang)

Maeuntang means spicy stew, and it originated from fishermen making soups with the fish parts left over after filleting their catch. It is often served as a combo dish to accompany hoe (sashimi) and Korean rice liquor (soju). You can use any type of whitefish; the most commonly used are cod and red snapper.

Cooking time: 1 hour Makes 4 to 6 servings

Get the fish cleaned at the fishmonger. It saves a lot of time and mess! Cut the fish into 3 or 4 pieces.

Pat the fish dry with paper towels, sprinkle all over with 1 tablespoon salt and set aside.

If you are using fresh clams that haven't been cleaned yet, soak them in plenty of cold water with a handful of salt for 3 hours to get the sand out, then rinse them clean. If you are using frozen clams, you can skip this step.

INGREDIENTS

1 (2-pound) whole cod or red snapper, scales, intestines and fins removed
1 tablespoon salt
10 ounces fresh or frozen littleneck clams
8 cups water
10 large dried anchovies
3 dried red chiles
1 (4-inch-square) dashima (dried kelp)
8 cloves garlic, minced
3 tablespoons Korean red chile flakes*
2 tablespoons gukganjang (light soy sauce)
1/3 medium daikon radish
4 fresh red or green chiles
1 (2-ounce) bundle ssukgat (edible chrysanthemums)** (see next page)
1 small leek, white and green parts
1 (3 1/2-ounce) package baby oyster mushrooms
1/2 (1-pound) package firm tofu
1/2 medium yellow onion
1 tablespoon soybean paste

THE BROTH

In a large pot over high heat, boil the water with the anchovies, dried red chiles, and dashima for 30 minutes.

*Dried Korean red chiles (marungochu) can be found in the dried goods section of Korean grocery stores. They are spicier than fresh red chiles and are often used in making spicy broth.

THE SAUCE

Mix the soy sauce, minced garlic, and chile flakes in a bowl. Set aside.

Prep the Veggies!

Wash and cut the daikon radish into chunky 1/2-inch-thick squares.

Cut the fresh chiles into chunky rings.

Wash the chrysanthemum leaves.

DISCARD

Wash the leek thoroughly to get all the dirt out, then cut it into 3-inch logs.

Cut off the roots of the baby oyster mushrooms and discard. Rinse the mushrooms clean.

**Chrysanthemum leaves have a delicate, herby, smoky taste. You can get them at Korean or Chinese grocery stores. If you can't find them, you can use mustard greens instead.

Cut the tofu into 1/2-inch-thick rectangles.

Cut the onion into chunky bite-size pieces.

Everything into the pot

In another medium pot, layer the daikon radish, onion, and fresh chiles on the bottom, then place the clams and fish on top. Pour in the hot broth and add the soybean paste. Boil over high heat for 15 minutes.

THE SAUCE

Then add the leek, tofu, mushrooms, and the sauce. Boil for 10 minutes.

Last, add the chrysanthemum leaves and turn off the heat. Now it's ready to eat!

ENJOY

Serve it in a warmed ttukbaegi (Korean earthenware pot) set on a portable gas burner to keep it bubbling hot throughout the meal.

Spicy Beef Soup

(Yukgaejang)

This rich, spicy soup is perfect for cold weather; it will warm you right up!

Cooking time: 1 hour 20 minutes Makes 4 to 6 servings

Let's make the broth and boil the beef! First, wash the daikon radish and leek. Peel the onion and garlic. Wash the beef in cold water and pat it dry with paper towels.

BUBBLE...

THE BROTH

INGREDIENTS

1 pound daikon radish
1 small leek, white and green parts, cut into 3-inch pieces
1 medium onion
16 cloves garlic
1 1/2 pounds beef brisket
12 cups water
1 (4-inch-square) dashima (dried kelp)
1 teaspoon peppercorns
2 tablespoons soju (Korean rice liquor)
7 tablespoons Korean red chile flakes
5 tablespoons gukganjang (light soy sauce)
1 tablespoon fish sauce
3 tablespoons toasted sesame oil, plus more for drizzling
5 ounces dangmyun (sweet potato noodles)
1 (3 1/2-ounce) package baby oyster mushrooms
3 green onions, white and green parts
8 ounces gosari (boiled fern)*
8 ounces mung bean sprouts
3 dried red chiles
2 eggs

In a large pot over high heat, combine the water with the daikon radish, leek, onion, dashima, 6 cloves of garlic, and the peppercorns. When the water boils, add the beef and the soju and turn down the heat to medium. Put the lid on the pot and boil for 40 minutes.

*Gosari is the young stems of brake ferns and have a meaty, stringy texture. You can find it already cleaned, boiled, and packaged in water in the refrigerated section of Korean grocery stores.

• THE SAUCE •

Crush the remaining 10 cloves of garlic and mix them with the chile flakes, soy sauce, fish sauce, and 1 tablespoon of sesame oil. Set aside.

생교사리
NET 1 lb
BOILED

Soak the sweet potato noodles in plenty of cold water for 30 minutes and drain.

Wash the baby oyster mushrooms and discard the roots. Cut the green onions into chunky logs.

DISCARD

Blanch the gosari and mung bean sprouts separately in boiling water for a couple of minutes and drain.

After 40 minutes of boiling!

Cut the beef into strips that are about 1/4 inch thick, 3 inches long, following the grain.

Cool the beef on a cutting board until it's cool enough to touch. Strain the broth and discard the rest of the ingredients in the pot.

SPICY~!

Add the sweet potato noodles to the pot. Crack the eggs into a bowl and whisk the yolks and the whites together.

Heat a pot over high heat with the remaining 2 tablespoons of sesame oil and dried red chiles.

Add the beef strips and gosari and sauté for 2 minutes. Take out the dried chiles and add the bean sprouts and mushrooms and pour the broth and the sauce into the pot. Boil for 15 minutes.

Slowly pour in the eggs as you stir the pot. Add the green onions and boil until the noodles are cooked, about 4 minutes.

Now it's done! Drizzle over some toasted sesame oil and salt and pepper to taste!

ENJOY!

Chapter 6
Porridges

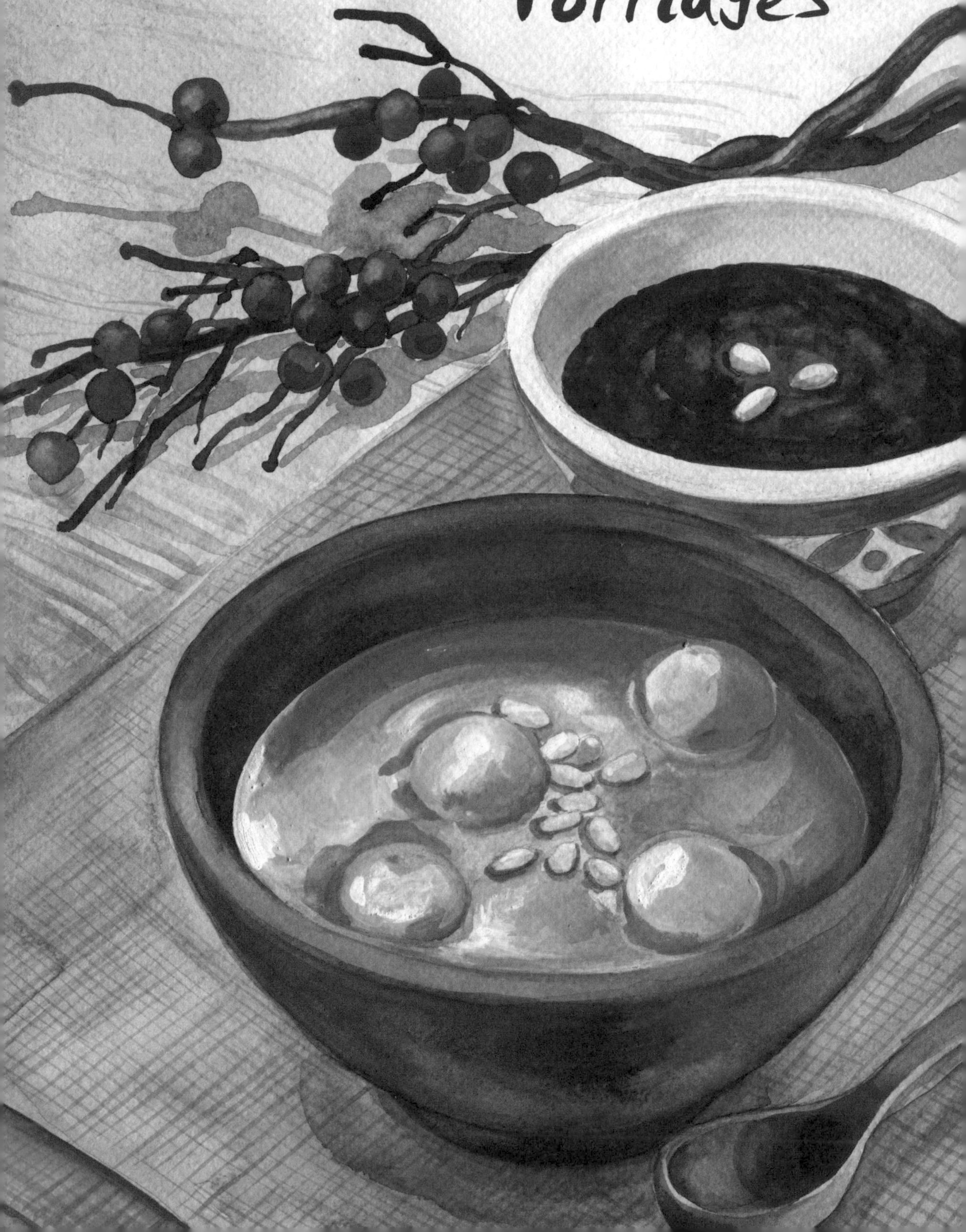

INTRO TO JUK

Korean porridge is called juk, and there are dozens of different kinds.

It is mainly made by cooking rice slowly over low heat with lots of water and then adding a variety of ingredients to it.

It is soft and easy to digest and often given to children, the elderly, and people recovering from illnesses.

No need to chew!

Healthy adults enjoy it, too, as a special pick me up.

There are two types of juk: sweet and savory. Sweet rice flour is sometimes added to thicken the porridge.

Red bean porridge with whole beans and rice kernels is served hot.

Smoothly blended sweet pumpkin porridge is served cold.

Small sticky rice balls called "ongsimi" are added for decoration and to give juk more substance.

Sweet porridges can be served warm or cold, and are garnished with pine nuts, jujubes, and pumpkin seeds with a drizzle of honey.

Savory porridges can range from delicate grits made with nutritious nuts and seeds, to hearty porridges made with seafood, veggies, or meats.

Toasted sesame seeds, crushed toasted seaweed, and toasted sesame oil are often added on top right before serving the savory porridges.

PINE NUT (Jatjuk) PORRIDGE

This porridge is like Korean grits, enhanced with the richness of pine nuts. Its smooth texture and mild flavor is great for children and adults alike.

Prep time: 2 hours Cooking time: 20 minutes Makes 2 or 3 servings

Soak the sweet rice in plenty of cold water for 2 hours. $\frac{1}{2}$ cup sweet rice will expand into $\frac{3}{4}$ cup of soaked rice.

Sweet rice is short grain rice that becomes very sticky when cooked. It's gluten-free and used to make sweet porridges. It can also be milled and pounded into rice cakes.

INGREDIENTS

$\frac{1}{2}$ cup sweet rice
1 cup milk
$\frac{1}{4}$ cup pine nuts, plus more for garnish
$1\frac{1}{2}$ cups water
Salt and freshly ground pepper
Pine needles, for garnish

Drain the sweet rice and blend it with the milk, then pour it into a pot.

Add the pine nuts and bring to a boil over high heat, then turn the heat down to medium.

In the empty blender, blend the pine nuts with $\frac{1}{2}$ cup of the water and pour it into the pot.

Add $\frac{1}{2}$ teaspoon of salt. Stir consistently for 10 to 15 minutes, until the porridge thickens.

Blend it very finely.

weee

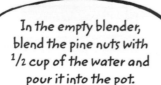

→ DISCARD then
← insert

Don't eat the pine needle! It's just for decoration.

Spear several pine nuts with pine needles for garnish. Season with salt and pepper to taste.

Add the remaining cup of water to the blender and pulse until the water swishes away all of the rice residue. Pour the water and rice residue into the pot.

ENJOY

BLACK SESAME porridge

(Heukimjajuk)

Black sesame seeds are often used in traditional Korean fine dining because of their delicate floral aroma and rich nutritional value. This is a savory porridge with a mildly bitter aftertaste.

Prep time: 2 hours Cooking time: 20 minutes Makes 3 or 4 servings

Soak the sushi rice in plenty of cold water for 2 hours, then drain.

1/2 a cup of rice will expand into 3/4 cup of soaked rice.

INGREDIENTS

1/2 cup sushi rice
1/4 cup raw black sesame seeds
3 1/2 cups water
1 teaspoon salt
Pine nuts, for garnish
Honey, for serving

In a blender, combine the soaked sushi rice and 2 1/2 cups of water and blend it coarse. Pour the blended rice into a pot. Add the remaining cup of water to the blender and pulse until the water swishes away all of the rice residue. Pour the water and rice residue into the pot.

Place the sesame seeds in a pan over medium heat and toast them for a few minutes, until they are crispy.

Heat the porridge over medium-low heat and add the ground sesame seeds and salt.

Stir for about 10 minutes, until the mixture thickens.

Let's eat!

Serve warm and garnish with pine nuts. Add honey to taste.

Finely grind the toasted sesame seeds in a spice grinder.

ENJOY

SWEET RED BEAN PORRIDGE

(Danpatjuk)

In Korea this porridge is traditionally eaten on the winter solstice because the red color of the beans is believed to restore positive energy and scare away evil spirits. You can use more or less sugar, depending on your taste.

Prep time: 2 hours Cooking time: 1 hour 15 minutes Makes 6 to 8 servings

Soak the sushi rice in plenty of water for 2 hours; it will expand to 3/4 cup of rice. Drain and set aside.

INGREDIENTS

1/2 cup sushi rice
1 cup dried red beans*
1/2 cup sweet rice flour
12 peeled cooked chestnuts**
  (see next page)
2 tablespoons brown sugar
1 teaspoon salt
Pine nuts, for garnish
Honey, for serving

*Dried red beans are sold at Asian grocery stores.

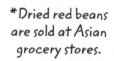

Rinse the red beans in cold running water.

Meanwhile... Let's make ONGSIMI!

Ongsimi is a small, chewy sticky rice ball served in Korean porridges. They're supereasy and fun to make.

In a large pot over high heat, combine the red beans with 10 cups of water and boil for 45 minutes.

MAKE the DOUGH

Put the sweet rice flour in a bowl and add 5 tablespoons of HOT water, 1 tablespoonful at a time and mix with a spoon until cool enough to touch.

Then knead the dough well with your hands.

When the dough has a Play-Doh-like consistency, take about a thumb-size lump.

Rub it between your palms to make a ball.

You'll be able to make about 20 little balls.

BACK TO THE BEANS~

After about 45 minutes, most of the water in the pot will have been absorbed by the beans.

Set aside about 1/2 a cup of cooked beans.

When you can easily smash the beans with a spoon, remove it from the heat.

Blend the rest of the beans, including the liquid in the pot, with 1 cup water until the texture is smooth and creamy.

All into the pot!

Combine the blended beans, reserved whole beans, drained sushi rice, ongsimi, chestnuts, brown sugar, and salt. Boil over medium-low heat for about 15 minutes.

**You can find peeled and cooked chestnuts in a can or pouch in most grocery shops.

Stir until the porridge thickens.

Ready to eat!

Danpatjuk can be served hot or cold. Add pine nuts and honey to taste.

ENJOY

sweet Pumpkin PORRIDGE
(Hobakjuk)

This is more of a sweet treat than a savory one. You can add more or less sugar, depending on your taste. It is usually served chilled.

Cooking time: 1 hour 15 minutes Makes 4 to 6 servings

*Kabocha squash is called danhobak in Korean, which means "sweet pumpkin." It's a common winter squash and it's easy to find in grocery stores in the fall. You can also use buttercup squash, which looks and tastes very similar.

INGREDIENTS

2 pounds kabocha squash*
5 cups water
1/3 cup sweet rice flour
20 ongsimi balls (page 108)
3 tablespoons brown sugar
3 tablespoons granulated sugar
1 teaspoon salt
Pine nuts, for garnish
Black sesame seeds, for garnish
1 dried red date (jujube),
   thinly sliced

Rinse any dirt off the outside of the squash and cut it into big chunky sections with a big knife.

Keep your fingers away from the knife!

CHAK!

Take out and discard all of the seeds.

Put the squash in a big pot and pour in enough water to cover. Boil for 20 to 25 minutes, with the lid on.

Poke the squash with a chopstick. If it goes in smoothly, it's done.

Poke

BUBBLE...

Take the squash out of the pot and let it cool.

When cool enough to touch, peel the skin off the squash.

Whisk the sweet rice flour with the remaining 1 cup of water.

SWEET RICE

Blend the squash with 4 cups of the water until smooth.

EVERYTHING goes into the pot!

Pour the blended squash into the pot and add the ongsimi and the sweet rice flour mixture. Bring to a boil, then lower the heat to medium.

Sprinkle with pine nuts, black sesame seeds, and the sliced date for garnish.

Add the brown sugar, granulated sugar, and salt. Cook, stirring, for about 15 minutes, until the soup becomes glossy and thickened.

ENJOY

Seafood ♥ Mushroom Porridge

(Haemul Beoseot Juk)

Here is my variation of the traditional abalone porridge called jeonbokjuk, replacing the abalone with inexpensive ingredients like mushrooms and frozen seafood mix (found in the refrigerated sections of most grocery stores).

Soaking time: 2 hours Cooking time: 30 minutes
Makes 4 to 6 servings

INGREDIENTS

3 king oyster mushrooms
2 cloves garlic, peeled
1/2 medium yellow onion
1 cup frozen seafood mix
1 cup sushi rice
3 tablespoons fish sauce
2 tablespoons toasted sesame oil,
   plus more for drizzling
5 cups water
4 to 6 eggs (1 per serving)
Toasted seaweed, for garnish
Toasted sesame seeds, for garnish
Salt

The king oyster mushroom is my favorite kind of mushroom. It's meaty and sweet, and it goes especially well with seafood.

Discard

Gently wipe off the dirt with a damp paper towel and cut off the root end of the mushrooms.

Then chop up the mushrooms into small bite-size pieces.

Mince the garlic.

And dice the onion into tiny pieces.

112

Defrost the seafood mix in the microwave for a minute.

Soak the rice in water for 2 hours and then drain.

Then put the seafood mix, rice, mushrooms, onion, and garlic in a pot with the fish sauce and toasted sesame oil. Sauté over high heat for about 5 minutes.

Add the 5 cups of water, and when it starts to boil, turn down the heat to medium-low and simmer for 20 minutes.

Stir often so the rice doesn't stick to the bottom of the pot.

Meanwhile... soft boil the eggs!

Put the eggs in a pot of boiling water. Put the lid on, turn down the heat to low, and simmer for 7 minutes.

Then dunk the eggs in ice-cold water for 3 minutes.

Peel the egg under cold running water, and you've got a perfectly soft-boiled egg.

The final Touch

Ladle the porridge into 4 to 6 bowls and put a soft-boiled egg on top. For garnish, cut the seaweed into strips and scatter over the top. Sprinkle with sesame seeds and drizzle with sesame oil.

Salt to taste as you eat.

ENJOY

Chapter 7
Noodles and Rice Cakes

INTRO TO NOODLES

Noodles are called myun or guksu in Korean, and there are dozens of different types in Korea. People used to make them at home from scratch back in the day, but there are so many fresh and inexpensive noodles available at grocery stores now that most people buy them. Here are some of the most common types you can find at Korean grocery stores.

DRIED NOODLES

막국수 (makguksu) or 소면 (somyun) are the thin white noodles made with wheat flour. They are very versatile and can be eaten either cold or in a hot soup. See Bibim Guksu on page 118.

당면 (dangmyun) are semitranslucent light brown noodles made with sweet potato flour. They are used to make Japchae (page 126) and are also added to stews to give more substance.

냉면 (naengmyun) are chewy and elastic noodles made with buckwheat flour. They are used to make the popular cold noodle soup called Mulnaengmyun (page 128).

메밀국수 (memilguksu) are thin gray noodles similar to the Japanese soba. They contain buckwheat and are eaten cold with a dipping sauce.

FRESH NOODLES

Most of the dried noodles are also available as fresh noodles in the refrigerated section of the grocery store. I prefer using fresh noodles for thick, doughy noodles such as jjajang and kalguksu.

우동 (udon) or 짜장 (jjajang) are thick round noodles used in Jjajangmyeon (page 166), jjamppong, and udon soups.

ROUND

칼국수 (kalguksu) are flat, starchy noodles traditionally made by cutting the dough with a knife (see page 124 and below).

FLAT

Handmade Knife Noodles Recipe

Mix 3½ cups all purpose flour, 1¼ cups lukewarm water, 1 teaspoon salt, and 1 teaspoon cooking oil in a large mixing bowl.

Cooking time: 30 minutes
Makes 4 servings

Knead the dough until you can form a smooth ball and wrap the doughball with a plastic wrap. Leave it for 20 minutes.

Divide the dough ball into quarters. Dust a large cutting board with flour, and knead each dough piece into a flat disk. Then roll the dough out with a rolling pin into a large, thin sheet about ⅛ inch thick.

Dust the top of the rolled out dough with flour and fold it a couple of times lengthwise, then cut it into about ¼-inch-thick strips.

RICE CAKE

떡 (tteok) comes in all shapes and sizes but all are essentially the same thing: glutinous rice pounded into a chewy, sticky dough. It is great as the substitute ingredient in noodle soups or as the starch component in stews. It is also eaten by itself or fried as a snack.

떡볶이떡 (tteokbokkitteok) is a smaller version of garetteok, mainly used in making the popular street food called Tteokbokki (page 132).

가래떡 (garetteok) is the most basic form of rice cake. It looks like a long white log. It tastes great when pan-fried and dipped in honey as a snack.

떡국떡 (tteokguk tteok) is diagonally sliced rice cake that is used to make a hot soup called Tteokguk (page 120).

There are dozens of different kinds of tteok. Most tteok are meant to be eaten as it is, like a snack or dessert. Here are a few kinds that are easy to find premade at Korean grocery stores, or at tteokjip, a store that specializes in making tteok.

송편 (songpyeon) is a half-moon shaped tteok that is traditionally eaten at chuseok, the Korean Thanksgiving. It has either sweet beans or chestnut paste, sugar and sesame seed paste, or savory whole bean fillings. It is steamed over pine needles which gives it the fragrance of pine trees and is often served with a garnish of pine needles.

백설기 (baekseolgi) is a semisweet and fluffy tteok that is traditionally eaten at a baby's first birthday. It usually comes in white with whole beans and dried fruit topping. The sweeter, multi-colored version with pink, yellow, and green strips are called mujigyetteok (rainbow rice cake).

인절미 (ingeolmi) is a sticky tteok that is soft, chewy and smothered in variations of a sweet and savory bean powder called gomul. It's a common tteok to eat during festivities like weddings and birthdays. When dipped in honey, this tteok is a great complement to a hot tea.

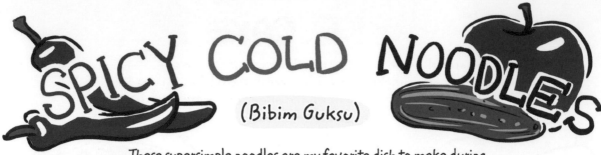

SPICY COLD NOODLES

(Bibim Guksu)

These supersimple noodles are my favorite dish to make during
the summer. If you want them less spicy, you can use less gochujang and
kimchi, substituting with a little bit more sugar, soy sauce, and lettuce.

Cooking time: 10 minutes Makes 2 servings

INGREDIENTS

4 large Romaine lettuce leaves
1 Kirby cucumber, unpeeled
1 cup kimchi (page 26)
1/4 small Fuji or Gala apple
3 tablespoons kimchi juice
3 tablespoons gochujang (red chile paste)
2 tablespoons rice vinegar
2 teaspoons sugar
1 tablespoon soy sauce
1 tablespoon toasted sesame oil
2 (3-ounce) bundles somyun or
　makguksu noodles
1 hard-boiled egg, halved
Toasted sesame seeds, for garnish
Toasted seaweed, crushed, for garnish
Tobiko (flying fish roe) for garnish (optional)

Somyun and makguksu are
thin white Korean wheat noodles.
They are as thin as angel-hair pasta.

Let's prep the veggies!

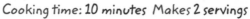

ROLL 'EM

DISCARD

Cut off the thick white bottoms of
the lettuce leaves. Roll the leaves into
a cigar shape and slice into thin ribbons.

Slice the cucumber into
thin matchsticks.

Cut the kimchi into
small bite-size
pieces.

Let's make the SAUCE!

Peel and chop the apple into bite-size pieces. In a blender, combine the apple with the kimchi juice, gochujang, vinegar, sugar, soy sauce, and sesame oil and blend into a smooth paste.

Traditionally, Asian pear is often used in this sauce. I've substituted it with apple, which is inexpensive and easier to find. You can also use pear, kiwi, or watermelon. If you don't have any fruit, no worries. Just add more kimchi juice and sugar instead!

Cook the somyun in boiling water for a couple of minutes and taste one to see if it's cooked. The noodle should be soft but still chewy and not mushy.

Rinse the cooked noodles with cold running water and drain.

Let's eat!

Spread the lettuce on the bottom of each of two serving bowls and put the noodles on top. Pour the sauce over the noodles and arrange the cucumber, kimchi, and a boiled egg half on top. Garnish with the toasted seaweed and sesame seeds. Tobiko is also a great garnish, if you want to add more exciting color and texture.

ENJOY

RICE CAKE SOUP
(Tteokguk)

In Korea, everyone marks another year of getting older by eating tteokguk on New Year's Day, no matter when their actual birthday is. The clean white color of the soup signals a fresh new start and the coin shape of the rice cakes is believed to bring good fortune and good luck. But, of course, you can enjoy this soup throughout the year for extra good luck!

Cooking time: 50 minutes Makes 4 servings

INGREDIENTS

1 pound rice cakes
8 ounces beef chuck
3 cloves garlic, peeled
3 green onions, white and green parts
1 tablespoon toasted sesame oil, plus more for drizzling
1 tablespoon gukganjang (light soy sauce)
1 tablespoon soju (Korean rice liquor)
2 egg yolks
Salt
2 teaspoons olive oil
Toasted seaweed, for garnish
Freshly ground pepper

First, soak the rice cakes in cold water for 20 minutes. Make sure that all the rice cake pieces are separated from each other.

Wash the beef with cold water and pat it dry with paper towels. Cut it into small bite-size pieces.

Crush the garlic and cut the green onions into thin slices.

Heat a pot over high heat with the toasted sesame oil and sauté the beef with the garlic, soy sauce, and soju.

When the beef is no longer pink, add 8 cups of water and boil over high heat for 15 minutes.

You will see a layer of brown foam bubbling on the top of the broth. With a large spoon, skim off as much of this as you can to make the broth clear. Drain the rice cakes that have been soaking in water and add them to the pot.

Boil for about 5 minutes.

Meanwhile...

Whisk 2 egg yolks with a pinch of salt and 1 tablespoon of water. Heat a pan over high heat with the oil and pour the egg mixture to make a thin omelet.

CUT

Cut the omelet into a square, then thinly slice the square into 2-inch strips.

Add the green onions and boil for another minute, then it's done!

ENJOY

Ladle the soup into bowls and drizzle with toasted sesame oil. Crush a little bit of toasted seaweed and add a few strips of the egg yolk for garnish. Season with salt and pepper to taste.

HAND-PULLED DOUGH ~SOUP~ with POTATOES

(Gamja Sujebi)

This rustic soup is a lot of fun to make with friends and family. It is the the most basic form of a noodle soup to which you can add any meat or vegetables to make it more substantial and interesting. Potatoes, shredded chicken, and kimchi are the most popular toppings for this dish.

Prep time: 1 hour 15 minutes   Cooking time: 50 minutes   Makes 4 to 6 servings

Let's make the DOUGH!

Mix the flour with the salt, then add the water and knead the dough with your hands for 10 to 15 minutes. When all of the flour is incorporated and the dough forms a nice, smooth ball, the dough is done.

Cover the dough in plastic wrap and chill it in the refrigerator for an hour.

INGREDIENTS

Dough
2 cups all-purpose flour
1 teaspoon salt
7/8 cup water

- - - - - - - - - - - - - -

Soup
12 cups water
5 dried shiitake mushrooms
1 (4-inch-square) dashima (dried kelp)
10 large dried anchovies, cleaned and put in a strainer ball (see page 97)
2 large yellow potatoes
1 large zucchini
1 medium yellow onion
3 green onions, white and green parts
3 cloves garlic, peeled
Toasted sesame oil, for drizzling
Salt and freshly ground pepper

Meanwhile...

Discard.

Let's make the soup. I'm making anchovy broth in this recipe but you can also use beef, chicken, or vegetable broth. Boil the water with the dried shiitake mushrooms, dried kelp, and the strainer ball of the dried anchovies for 30 minutes.

Wash all of the vegetables and peel the potatoes. Dice the potatoes, zucchini, and yellow onion into bite-size pieces, about 1/4 inch thick. Chop the green onions into 3-inch pieces and mince the garlic.

Discard the anchovies and the kelp. Take out the shiitake mushrooms and set them aside.

Add the potatoes, onion, and garlic to the pot and boil for 10 minutes.

When the shiitake mushrooms are cool enough to touch,

discard the stems, cut the mushrooms into thin strips, and add them into the pot along with the zucchini.

Let's make the dough flakes!

It's so sticky!

Having extra hands would make this process much quicker and more fun!

Make 1 1/4-inch-thick, bite-size flakes and toss them into the pot. Don't worry about the irregular shapes. That's part of the charm!

Moistening your fingers with water makes it easier to work with sticky dough.

Toss

Close the lid and cook the dough flakes until they float to the top.

My dough flake looks like a heart!

Last, add the green onions and boil for a minute.

Drizzle with some toasted sesame oil and season with salt and pepper to taste.

ENJOY

KNIFE  NOODLE
SOUP with CLAMS
(Bajirak Kalguksu)

Kalguku means knife noodle, which is traditionally made by cutting homemade dough with a knife. This recipe uses the premade noodles that you can find in the refrigerated section of the Korean grocery stores. Or you can make your own noodles by following the recipe on page 116.

Cooking time: 45 minutes   Makes 2 or 3 servings

INGREDIENTS

2 (7-ounce) bundles kalguksu noodles
10 fresh or frozen littleneck clams
10 large dried anchovies
1 (4-inch-square) dashima
   (dried kelp)
2 medium yellow potatoes
1 medium yellow onion
1 small zucchini
1 Korean red chile pepper
3 cloves garlic, peeled
3 green onions, white and green
   parts, plus thinly sliced green
   onions for garnish
2 tablespoons gukganjang
   (light soy sauce)
Toasted sesame oil, for drizzling
Salt and freshly ground pepper

A Perfect Vessel!

Kalguksu noodles go well with any meat, seafood or vegetables just like linguine in Italian cooking. Littleneck clams are my favorite ingredient to put into this noodle soup, but you can substitute shredded beef, chicken, or kimchi.

A HANDFUL OF SALT

If you are using fresh clams, make sure you soak them in salt water for 3 hours. Then rinse them in cold water to get the sand out.

OR →

If you want to skip this process, use frozen clams.

Boil 8 cups of water with the dried anchovies and dried kelp to make the broth.

Discard the head and guts of the dried anchovies and put them in a strainer ball.

Boil for 20 minutes over high heat, then discard the anchovies and the kelp.

Meanwhile...

Peel and dice the potatoes and onion into about 1-inch cubes. Julienne the zucchini, and cut the red chile pepper into chunky rings. Mince the garlic. Cut the green onions into 3-inch pieces and chop the rest for garnish.

Add the littleneck clams, potatoes, onion, garlic, and soy sauce to the pot.

Boil over high heat for 15 minutes.

The premade kalguksu noodles are covered in loose flour to keep them from sticking to each other. Untangle the noodles and rinse off the flour in cold running water before adding it to the pot so the broth doesn't get thick and goopy.

Put the rinsed noodles, zucchini, green onion pieces, and red chile into the pot.

LAST...

Boil for about 5 minutes until the noodles and zucchini are cooked al dente.

Season with salt and pepper to taste.

Drizzle with toasted sesame oil and sprinkle the chopped green onions on top before serving.

ENJOY

125

Feast for your eyes, party in your mouth!

SWEET POTATO NOODLES (Japchae)

These versatile noodles taste great hot or cold. This is a good dish to bring to potlucks or picnics. You can substitute chicken, pork, or tofu for the beef.

Cooking time: 30 minutes Makes 4 to 6 servings

Japchae is the quintessential party food in Korea, and it's usually made in big batches. This is why dangmyun comes in a huge, long bundle, which can make it challenging to separate just a small amount.

Once you get the noodles out of the package, soak them in plenty of cold water.

INGREDIENTS

8 ounces dangmyun (dried sweet potato noodles)
1/2 red bell pepper
1 medium carrot, peeled
1 medium yellow onion
2 ounces fresh shiitake mushrooms
3 green onions, white and green parts
4 cloves garlic, peeled
8 ounces lean beef (chuck shoulder, sirloin steak, or eye round)
2 tablespoons olive oil
1 tablespoon sugar
1 tablespoon soju (Korean rice liquor)
3 tablespoons soy sauce
4 ounces spinach
Salt and freshly ground pepper
1 tablespoon toasted sesame oil
1 teaspoon toasted sesame seeds

Let's prep the Veggies!

Cut the red bell pepper, carrot, yellow onion, and shiitake mushrooms into thin strips.

DISCARD the stems

SO Colorful

Cut the green onions into 3-inch pieces.

Mince the garlic.

Cut the beef into thin strips

about 1/2 inch wide.

Heat up a pan with 1 tablespoon of the oil over high heat and cook the meat with the garlic, onion, sugar, soju, and 1 tablespoon of the soy sauce.

When the onion is translucent and the meat is well done, transfer them to a bowl and set aside.

In the same pan, heat up 1 tablespoon of oil and sauté the carrot, shiitake mushrooms, and red bell pepper. When the crunchiness of the carrot is gone, add the green onions and cook for a couple more minutes. Season with salt and pepper to taste.

Meanwhile...

Boil a pot of water big enough for the dangmyun noodles. When it simmers, blanch the spinach for about 20 seconds.

Remove the blanched spinach from the water, cool, and squeeze out the water. Set the spinach aside.

In the same pot of water, boil the soaked and untangled dangmyun for about 6 minutes. Drain them and put them in a big mixing bowl.

All together!

Combine the noodles, meat, all of the vegetables, the remaining 2 tablespoons soy sauce, toasted sesame oil, and toasted sesame seeds. Season with salt and pepper to taste.

Cut the noodles with scissors before serving, if they are still too tangled.

ENJOY

COLD BUCKWHEAT noodles
(Mulnaengmyun)

Mulnaengmyun means water cold noodles. These cold noodles are very chewy and have the elasticity of rubber bands. You can enjoy the broth without adding any spice to it, or you can add Korean yellow wasabi paste (yengyeoja) or chile bibim sauce for a kick. You can also eat these noodles without the broth, just with chile bibim sauce instead. The brothless version is called bibimnaengmyun, which means cold noodles mixed in sauce.

Prep time: 2 hours 30 minutes Cooking time: 10 minutes Makes 4 servings

The key to delicious mulnaengmyun is in the broth, and it's very easy to make! Boil 6 cups of water with 1 teaspoon of salt and blanch the beef brisket for about a minute until it's no longer pink.

Let the brisket cool, then put on a plate, cover with plastic wrap and chill it in the refrigerator for 2 hours.

Chill the broth in the refrigerator for 2 hours

Let's make the pickle.

INGREDIENTS

10 cups water
Salt
8 ounces beef brisket, thinly sliced
2 Kirby cucumbers, cut into matchsticks
1/2 small daikon radish, cut into matchsticks
6 tablespoons sugar
1 1/4 cup rice vinegar
1 (1-pound) package naengmyun (dried buckwheat noodles)
3/4 medium Asian pear, peeled and cut into thin wedges
2 hard-boiled eggs, halved
Yengyeoja (Korean yellow wasabi paste*), for serving (see next page)

- -

Chile Bibim Sauce
1/4 medium Asian pear, peeled and chopped
1/4 small yellow onion, chopped
1 clove garlic, chopped
1 1/4 cup gochujang (red chile paste)
3 tablespoons soy sauce
3 tablespoons rice vinegar
2 tablespoons toasted sesame oil
1 tablespoon Korean red chile flakes
2 teaspoons toasted sesame seeds
1 teaspoon sugar

In a mixing bowl, combine the cucumber and daikon radish with sugar, vinegar, and 2 tablespoons of salt.

Set it aside for 10 minutes.

Pack the cucumber and daikon radish into a jar along with the brine and add the remaining 4 cups of water.

Cover, and chill it in the refrigerator for 2 hours.

So easy!

2 HOURS LATER...

Take out the broth from the refrigerator and skim and discard the layer of fat on top of the broth.

Then put the broth in the freezer for extra coldness.

Cook the noodles in boiling water for about 3 minutes, until they become soft.

Drain the noodles and rinse them in cold running water.

Let's assemble!

In each bowl, combine 1 cup of chilled beef broth and 1 cup of the pickle juice and add the noodles. Arrange the cucumber and radish pickles, sliced Asian pear, beef briskets, and a hard-boiled egg on top.

Add the chile bibim sauce or Korean yellow wasabi paste to your taste. Add a couple of ice cubes to the soup to keep it extra cold throughout your meal.

THE CHILE BIBIM SAUCE

In a blender, puree the Asian pear, onion, and garlic and mix it with the chile paste, soy sauce, vinegar, sesame oil, chile flakes, sesame seeds, and sugar.

*Korean yellow wasabi paste is available at Korean grocery stores.

ENJOY

Chapter 8
Snacks and Street Food

INTRO TO BUNSIK

Bunsik means food made with flour—they are EVERYWHERE in Korea.

Fries of all kinds

Sweet bean waffles

Gimbap

Fried spicy rice cakes

Boiled snails

Steamed buns

Blood sausages

Pancakes

Spicy rice cakes

Dumplings

Korean cities are full of street vendors selling all kinds of bunsik. The word bunsik can also refer to street snacks or on-the-go-food.

Streets aren't the only place to find bunsik. You can find some of the best bunsik in Korea at. . . .

Rest stops

Amusement parks

Movie theaters

Ski resorts

Koreans take on-the-go-food to the next level. We love to hike, and instead of carrying granola bars in our backpacks, we carry all kinds of bunsik, side dishes, snacks, and even rice, including a portable burner to make freshly cooked rice.

Most fishing boats in Korea also carry portable burners and the essential ingredients to make a hot meal with their fresh catch right on the boat.

The best reward for a hard climb is to eat a hot delicious meal on the mountaintop.

From mountaintops to the tops of ocean waves, everywhere is a great place to eat in Korea.

SPICY RICE CAKES

(Tteokbokki)

This common Korean street food is especially popular with school kids. The thick sweet chile sauce is great for smothering other street food, like gimbap (page 142) and dumplings. If you don't want it spicy, substitue soy sauce and extra sugar for the gochujang.

Cooking time: 1 hour Makes 4 to 6 servings

Tteokbokki is usually made with the finger-size, tube-shaped white rice cake, but you can also use the diagonally sliced rice cake.

Soak the rice cake in plenty of cold water and set aside.

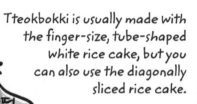

INGREDIENTS

1 pound rice cake
10 large dried anchovies
1 (4-inch-square) dashima (dried kelp)
10 ounces green cabbage
1 medium carrot, peeled
3 cloves garlic, peeled
3 green onions, white and green parts
4 sheets fish cake (see page 80)
1/3 cup gochujang (red chile paste)
2 tablespoons sugar
1 to 2 tablespoons Korean red chile flakes
1 teaspoon fish sauce
4 hard-boiled eggs, peeled and halved

Now, Let's make the Broth!

Discard the heads and guts of the dried anchovies.

Put the anchovies in a big strainer ball.

Boil 4 cups of water with the dried anchovies and dried kelp for 30 minutes.

Chop the cabbage into strips less than 1 inch wide.

Slice the carrot into thin diagonal coins and mince the garlic. Cut the green onions into 3-inch logs.

Cut the fish cake into 2-by-1-inch squares. Remove and discard the anchovies and kelp. Add the rice cake, fish cake, garlic, chile paste, sugar, 1 to 2 tablespoons of chile flakes, and fish sauce depending on how spicy you want it.

Make sure the pieces of rice cake are all separated from each other.

RED CHILE PASTE

SUGAR

SH CE

Boil for about 10 minutes. Stir occasionally so the rice cake doesn't get stuck to the bottom.

→ Discard

When the rice cake is cooked to al dente, add the cabbage and carrot to the pot and boil for about 10 minutes, until they are soft.

The Deluxe Versions

You can add dangmyun (sweet potato noodles) or ramen noodles with some water and boil for a few more minutes at the end.

Last, add the green onions to the pot along with the hard-boiled eggs.

Boil for a couple more minutes and it's done!

ENJOY

133

BROWN SUGAR pancakes

(Hotteok)

ooey Gooey~

This popular street food is served hot right out of the pan. Watch out for the burst of melted brown sugar that oozes out of the pocket when you take the first bite.

Prep time: 2 hours 45 minutes Cooking time: 30 minutes Makes 8 pancakes

INGREDIENTS

1 cup all-purpose flour
1 cup sweet rice flour
1 packet active dry yeast
  (3 teaspoons)
1 tablespoon sugar
1 teaspoon salt
1 cup milk
Olive oil, for cooking

Filling
1/2 cup firmly packed brown sugar
1/2 cup crushed nuts (such as
  peanuts, pine nuts, and walnuts)
1 teaspoon ground cinnamon
1 teaspoon salt

Let's make the batter! First, mix all-purpose flour, sweet rice flour, yeast, sugar, and salt.

In a cup, microwave the milk until it's lukewarm, 15 to 20 seconds.

Pour the milk into the dry ingredients and add 1 teaspoon of oil. Mix well, cover the bowl with a plastic wrap, and leave it someplace warm, like near a heating vent or in a turned off gas oven for 1 1/2 hours.

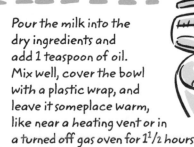

Remove the plastic wrap to check if the dough has risen. Stir the dough with a spoon. Re-cover with plastic wrap and leave it to rise some place warm for another hour.

134

Fluff the dough with a spoon again. Now it's time to make the hotteok! Wear disposable food prep gloves with some oil rubbed on them to keep your hands from sticking to the dough.

the filling

Mix the brown sugar, crushed nuts, ground cinnamon, and salt.

Oil for the hands

Divide the dough into 8 pieces. Take 1 piece of the dough in your palm, roll it into a ball, then flatten it with your palms.

Put a tablespoon of the filling in the middle of the dough. Gently pack it in with the back of a spoon and add another spoonful if you can.

PUSH in

Pull in the dough from all sides and close it up, sealing in the filling. Rub some more oil on your gloves and keep making these balls until all the dough and filling are gone.

Try experimenting with different fillings.

Heat a frying pan with plenty of oil. Put in 2 dough balls and gently press them down with a spatula. After about 15 seconds, flip them over and cook until both sides are golden brown.

Tik Tok

Chrr...

nutella

Peanut Butter

JAM

MOZZARELLA

TOMATO

Serve hot!

ENJOY!

135

BROWN · SUGAR
STICKY RICE
(Yaksik)

Yaksik means medicine food; it is packed with nutritious nuts and fruits. It's like the Korean version of energy bars! It is traditionally eaten on the first full moon of the year and also at weddings and on elderly people's birthdays.

Prep time: Overnight Cooking time: 20 minutes Makes 10 servings

Yaksik is one of the oldest Korean sweets; there are records of royalty eating it back in the thirteenth century.

King Soji of Shilla

Yum~♡

INGREDIENTS

2 cups sweet rice
$1\frac{1}{3}$ cups water
3 tablespoons soy sauce
2 tablespoons toasted sesame oil
1 teaspoon ground cinnamon
$\frac{3}{4}$ cup firmly packed brown sugar
$\frac{1}{2}$ cup dried red dates (jujubes)
$\frac{1}{2}$ cup peeled cooked chestnuts
$\frac{1}{4}$ cup crushed walnuts
2 tablespoons pine nuts

It was a rare treat for common people back then, because sugar was scarce in Korea. But nowadays everyone can enjoy it.

First, soak the sweet rice in plenty of water overnight; it will expand to 4 cups by the next day. Drain it and put it in a large microwave-safe casserole dish with the $1\frac{1}{3}$ cups water.

GO Electric!

Traditionally, yaksik is made in a big steamer using cheesecloth to hold the grains together, but that takes a lot of time and effort.

Some people these days use a pressure cooker or microwave instead. We use the microwave in this recipe!

Mix the rice thoroughly with water.

If the container comes with a lid, put the lid on it. If not, cover with plastic wrap and poke a few holes in the plastic.

Microwave for 10 minutes.

meanwhile...

Let's make the sauce! Mix the brown sugar, soy sauce, sesame oil, and cinnamon in a bowl.

Cut open the dried red dates and remove the seeds...

...and cut them into small bite-size pieces.

10 minutes later...

Be careful removing the plastic wrap, it might be HOT!

Add the sauce, dried red dates, chestnuts, walnuts, and pine nuts to the sweet rice and mix well. Put the lid or plastic wrap back on, microwave for another 10 minutes on high, and it's done!

Spread out the yaksik into a 1-inch-thick layer on a large baking sheet and let cool. Cut it into 2-inch squares for serving. You can store yaksik in the freezer for months, if it is sealed properly. Just defrost it in the microwave for about 20 seconds before serving and it's as good as new!

ENJOY

KIMCHI FRIED RICE

(Kimchi Bokkumbap)

Bokkumbap means fried rice, and there are many varieties. This is my go-to dish when I don't have much time or a lot of ingredients but want a superquick and yummy meal. You can substitute any kind of meat for the pork, even canned processed meat like tuna or Spam.

Cooking time: 20 minutes Makes 4 servings

CHOP CHOP!

Let's wash all of the vegetables and cut the onion and carrot into 1/4-inch pieces.

INGREDIENTS

1 medium yellow onion
1 small carrot, peeled
3 green onions, white and green parts, plus thinly sliced green onion for garnish
8 ounces pork belly
2 cups kimchi
1 tablespoon olive oil
1 teaspoon soju (Korean rice liquor)
Salt and freshly ground pepper
3 cups freshly cooked rice (page 18)
2 tablespoons kimchi juice
1 tablespoon butter
1 teaspoon sugar
1 tablespoon toasted sesame oil
4 fried eggs (1 per serving)
Toasted sesame seeds, for garnish
Toasted seaweed, crushed for garnish

Thinly slice the green onions.

Dice the pork belly into small bite-size cubes too.

Cut the kimchi into 1/2-inch-long bite-size pieces.

Heat up a wok with the oil and cook the pork belly with the soju and a pinch of salt and pepper for a minute. Then add the onion and carrot and sauté for another minute.

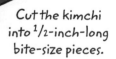

YUM~♡ SMELLS SO good!

Add the kimchi and sauté for a couple of minutes, until the onion and kimchi become soft and semitranslucent. Then add the cooked rice, kimchi juice, butter, and sugar and mix everything well. Sauté for about 5 more minutes.

SESAME OIL

Turn off the heat and add the toasted sesame oil and green onions. Mix well.

Serve it with a fried egg on top of each serving and sprinkle with green onion, toasted sesame seeds, and crushed toasted seaweed for garnish.

A side of pickled radish goes well with kimchi bokkumbap.

ENJOY!

BONUS ✶ RECIPE
PICKLED RADISH
(Tongdakmu)

This pickled radish is always served with Korean fried chicken, so no wonder it's called tongdakmu, meaning chicken radish. It goes well with any spicy fried dish and it's supereasy to make.

Wash and dice 1½ pounds of peeled daikon radish and cut it into ½-inch-cubes.

Soak the radish cubes in a mixture of ½ cup sugar, ¼ cup salt and ¼ cup rice vinegar for 10 minutes.

SUGAR

Add 1 cup of water and store the radish in the refrigerator overnight, then it's ready to eat!

Traditionally, we make this dish in a thick clay pot called a ttukbaegi, which might be a bit hard to find. So I've revised this recipe to use a regular earthenware bowl. Any ceramic soup or cereal bowl will also work.

Ttukbaegi (뚝배기)

♡ Korean Comfort ♡

egg in a Bowl

(Gyeranjjim)

If you want some variety in your egg repertoire, try this simple recipe. It is kind of like a steamed scrambled egg.

Cooking time: 20 minutes   Makes 1 or 2 servings

INGREDIENTS

2 large eggs
1/3 cup milk
Salt
1 green onion, green part only

MILK

Make sure the bowl is microwave and dishwasher safe.

Crack!

the eggs into a mixing bowl and add the milk and a pinch of salt.

Tok

Whisk

. . . until the yolk and white are well blended.

Pour the egg through a strainer into the earthenware bowl. This process makes the egg's texture smoother.

140

Thinly slice the green onion and add it to the eggs.

Cover the bowl with plastic wrap and poke a few holes on it.

pok

Fill the bottom of a pot with water, then place the bowl in the pot.

Cover the pot, bring the water to a boil and steam over high heat...

...for 15 to 20 minutes, until the egg becomes firm like soft tofu.

Now it's ready to eat!

ENJOY!

COLORFUL & Pretty~ SEAWEED RICE ROLL

(Gimbap)

SO Yummy~

Gimbap means seaweed rice, and it is the most common picnic food in Korea. Kimchi, bulgogi, and tuna salad are some of the popular ingredients to put inside the roll. You can also experiment and find your favorite combo. Bacon, fried chicken, and avocado? Roll' em all!

Cooking time: 1 hour Makes 7 rolls

Make sure you get the seaweed (gim) for rolling gimbap or sushi, NOT the usual toasted and seasoned kind. Gimbap seaweed is thicker and strong enough to keep all of the ingredients together in a roll.

About 10 inches

by 8 inches

INGREDIENTS

7 sheets dried seaweed for gimbap or sushi
1 large gimbap sausage
1 log danmuji (yellow pickled radish)
4 cups freshly cooked white rice (page 18)
Salt
2 tablespoons toasted sesame oil, plus more for cooking
2 teaspoons toasted sesame seeds
3 eggs
1 tablespoon olive oil
1 bunch of spinach, stemmed
1 large carrot, cut into thin matchsticks

Gimbap is so popular that Korean grocery stores sell a special sausage for gimbap; it is a large pink tube. Cut it lengthwise into 1/2-inch strips.

PICKLED RADISH 단무지

김밥용 단무지

Danmuji is a Korean pickled yellow radish. You can buy it as a large uncut log and cut it into 1/2-inch strips, or buy it already cut for making gimbap.

Beef Franks

You can also use beef franks or ham instead.

Set aside a large spoonful of the freshly cooked rice, then mix the rest with 1/2 teaspoon salt, 1 tablespoon toasted sesame oil, and a pinch of sesame seeds. Set aside to cool.

Saved plain rice.

Crack 3 eggs into a bowl and whisk together with 2 tablespoons of water and a pinch of salt.

Heat up a large pan with 1 tablespoon oil over medium-high heat. Pour the eggs into the pan and spread into a thin layer. Cook for a minute, then flip the omelet and cook the other side for about 2 minutes.

Assemble the FILLINGS!

Blanch the spinach for 30 seconds. Drain it and cool.

Squeeze out as much water as you can.

Then season it with 1/2 teaspoon salt and 1/2 teaspoon sesame oil.

Sauté sausage strips in a pan for a minute to brown the edges.

Transfer the omelet to a cutting board and and cut it into long 1/2-inch strips.

Strips of danmuji (pickled yellow radish)

A small dish of toasted sesame oil.

Sauté the carrot with a dash of sesame oil and 1/2 teaspoon salt.

(continued on next page)

TIME TO ROLL 'EM UP!

1 Place a sheet of seaweed on a bamboo sushi mat.

One side of the seaweed is shinier. Put the shiny side down, the rougher, dull side should face up.

2 Take about 1/2 cup of the seasoned rice.

Spread it evenly on the bottom half of the seaweed.

3 Place one line of each filling (see page 143) on top of the rice.

4

The plain, unseasoned rice acts as a glue.

Pick up the bottom edge of the sushi mat with both hands and roll it halfway, tucking everything in with your fingertips. Smear some of the reserved rice on the top edge.

5 Roll it all the way to the top and give it a firm squeeze.

6 Smear some toasted sesame oil on the finished roll to prevent it from sticking to the other rolls and put it on a wire rack or a large woven basket.

Shiny~

7 When all of the rolls are made,

cut them into 10–12 pieces with a sharp serrated knife.

8

Serve the rolls with some extra pieces of danmuji!

ENJOY

BBOPKI

is wafer-thin sugar candy. Swarms of kids would surround the bbopki maker after school in Korea, licking gingerly around the stamped-out marks on bbopki because...

...if you eat around the stamp without breaking it, you get another bbopki for free!

Some kids were good at it. I wasn't one of them.

Yay! I did it!

This is my third free bbopki. I'm gonna take it home for later.

Aww, man!

One day I broke one too many bbopki in a row and got so frustrated that I decided to try making it at home so I could practice eating around the stamps.

The bbopki maker was using two cans of white powder.

SUGAR

BAKING POWDER

What is baking powder? I've never heard of it but I must find it!

I found the baking powder at the local grocery shop.

I'll show those kids who's boss!!

Hehe...

I got right to making bbopki at home.

But it wasn't as easy as it looked.

Ack, I burned another one!

Chrr

It hardens before I even pour it onto the plate!

I finally got one right after burning all the ladles in the house.

HOW TO MAKE BBOPKI

Whisk 2 tablespoons of granulated sugar with a pinch of baking powder over high heat until it melts.

Pour it onto a flat surface. Press down with the bottom of a large plate. Stamp a cookie cutter on it and let it cool.

You're banned from making bbopki ever again!

Later that night...

WOOSH!

Alas, I never got the chance to master the art of licking bbopki stamps.

Chapter 9
Cocktails and Anju

Intro To Korean Drinking Culture

Koreans have been called the Irish of Asia, because guess what? We drink a lot!

Everything from important business deals to funerals happens over drinks in Korea.

There are three unspoken rules of drinking in Korea.

Rule #1 Always pour your elder's drink with both your hands.

One hand supports the other.

Some of these rules come from the traditional Confucian principles of respecting your elders.

Rule #2

Never refuse a drink from your elders. Receive your drink with both hands and drink it facing away from your elder.

Elder

Youth

After finishing your drink, offer a drink to the elder in return.

Rule #3

Always refill drinks for others and never refill your own drink. You must wait for the others to fill it up for you.

Let me pour it for you. It's bad luck to pour your own!

It encourages everyone to pay attention to each other.

Gunbae (cheers)!

CLANK!

Thus, everyone gets drunk at a steady and even pace.

Sul means liquor in Korean. The two most popular Korean liquors are soju and makgeolli.

Soju is a clear liquor made with rice, barley, and potato. It is about 20 percent alcohol and tastes similar to vodka. It is drunk by itself or in cocktails.

Makgeolli is an unfiltered rice wine with about 5 percent alcohol. It's mildly sweet and effervescent.

It used to be known as a farmer's drink, but it became trendy among young Koreans recently. You can find many bars that specialize in micro-brews of makgeolli in Korea.

Somek is short for soju and maekju (beer). It's a popular mixed drink made with a pint of beer and a shot of soju.

It is also called poktanju which means drink bomb, because it gets you drunk before you know it.

Watermelon Soju
(Subak Soju)

This is my favorite summer cocktail. The naturally sweet flavor of watermelon masks the alcoholic taste of soju, and the fun way it's served makes this cocktail a crowd pleaser at any party. It's also supersimple to make.

Cooking time: 10 minutes Makes 8 cups

First!

Halve a watermelon. You can reserve the other half for a refill as your party progresses.

INGREDIENTS

1 large seedless watermelon
1 (375-milliliter) bottle soju (Korean rice liquor)
2 cups Sprite
Ice cubes

PUSH!!

Cut about a quarter-inch off of the bottom of the watermelon half to make it flat.

Be careful not to scoop too close to the rind; keep a good 1-inch-thick wall so you don't accidentally make a hole.

1-inch

Hollow out the center of the watermelon half with a spoon and remove the seeds if there are any.

A flat bottom makes the watermelon stable enough to stand on its own.

Chill the scooped out flesh in the refrigerator for 1 hour.

Blend 3 cups watermelon with the soju, Sprite, and a cup of ice. Reserve some bite-size pieces.

Pour the blended mixture back into the watermelon rind bowl and float a handful of ice cubes and bite-size pieces of watermelon.

This cocktail tastes so refreshing on a hot summer day that it's easy to gulp down. It's deceptively strong, so pace your drinking!

Ready to DRINK!

ENJOY

Persimmon ~ Red Date punch

(Sujeonggwa)

Sujeonggwa is a traditional Korean nonalcoholic digestif. Its sweet and spicy aroma of ginger, cinnamon, and persimmon goes amazingly well with bourbon or whiskey. I've also included a cocktail version of this drink to add to the holiday bar menu.

Cooking time: 1 hour Makes 8 cups

What makes this punch taste so special is the warm, natural sweetness from dried persimmon (gotgam) and dried red dates (jujubes).

You can get both at Korean grocery stores in the fall.

INGREDIENTS

1 (1-inch) piece fresh ginger
8 cups water
1/2 cup sugar
6 sticks cinnamon
10 dried red dates (jujubes)
4 dried persimmons (gotgam)

Sugar was scarce in Korea back in the day, so natural sweets like dried persimmon and red dates were prized items and only used in fine dining.

The white powder on the surface of dried persimmons is a natural fungus that grows during the drying process. It's fine to eat.

Red dates (jujubes) are believed to have medicinal qualities and are used in many Korean fine dining and health food recipes.

Sac.

First!

Wash the ginger and scrape off the skin with a spoon.

Boil the water with ginger, sugar, cinnamon sticks, and dried red dates in a big pot.

Boil for 20 minutes over medium heat, then turn off the heat.

Discard the persimmon stems. If you are making a cocktail with the punch, save one persimmon for garnish and cut the rest of them into quarters. (Otherwise, quarter all the persimmons.)

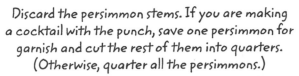

Discard ←

Take the ginger out of the pot and add the persimmon quarters.

Set aside to cool.

Take everything out of the pot and strain the liquid using a strainer lined with a coffee filter or a cheesecloth.

To avoid spilling, slowly pour the liquid cup by cup instead of trying to pour the whole pot all at once.

The punch is now done. Chill it in the refrigerator before serving.

Cocktail Garnish

If you are making cocktails with the punch, make this garnish. Make a slit on one side of the remaining persimmon and unroll it into a long strip.

Place a row of walnut halves on one side and roll the persimmon back into its original shape.

Cut the rolled up persimmon into 1/2-inch-thick rings.

TA-DA!

Sujeonggwa Cocktail

Mix 1 ounce of bourbon or whiskey with 3 ounces of punch.

ENJOY

Float a walnut persimmon ring and a few pine nuts for garnish.

Yogurt SOJU

(Yakult Soju)

This is probably the easiest and tastiest soju cocktail to make.
Makes 5 cups

INGREDIENTS

1 (375-milliliter) bottle soju
(Korean rice liquor)
5 (63-milliliter) bottles Yakult
2 cups Sprite
1 cup ice cubes

Yakult is a probiotic dairy drink made from skim milk.
It's popular throughout Asia and often served at
Korean restaurants as a complimentary dessert.
You can find it at Korean grocery stores.

Pour the soju, Yakult, and
Sprite into a pitcher
with the ice.

Mix well.
It's ready to drink!

ENJOY

152

INTRO TO ANJU

Anju refers to snacks or food that accompany alcoholic beverages.

Koreans always eat while drinking, because eating makes drinking more fun, and it protects you from getting drunk too fast and suffering from a hangover.

All anju are served family style to be shared with everyone.

Marun anju are dried snacks such as fish jerky, nuts, and rice crackers. Dried snacks and fruits are often served as anju when drinking Western liquors such as whiskey or vodka.

The most popular anju for beer is fried chicken. Koreans call this combo chimek—short for chicken and maekju (beer).

There are countless bars in Korea that specialize in chimek, and in recent years many of them have appeared in the U.S.

Fritters (twigim) and pancakes (jeon) can accompany all alcoholic drinks, from beers to Korean rice wine (makgeolli).

Pop-up tent bars called pojangmacha line the busy streets of Korean cities.

They are great, inexpensive places to drink for everyone from working-class Koreans to young professionals.

The popular drink and anju at pojangmacha are soju and fish cake soup, mussel soup, or army stew (Budaejjigae, page 154).

They are served on a portable burner to keep your food bubbling hot while you are drinking.

You can also find delicacies like chicken gizzards, chicken feet, and seafood at these little joints.

There is no limit to what can be called anju as long as you eat it with alcoholic drinks.

ARMY ★ STEW
(Budaejjigae)

BUBBLE

This hybrid of American and Korean fast food originated during the Korean War, when the U.S. Army brought processed meats and canned goods into Korea. People began mixing together whatever food was available during wartime. Despite its unfortunate origins, budaejjigae has become one of the most beloved shared dishes of young bar patrons in modern Korea.

Cooking time: 30 minutes Makes 4 to 6 servings

There's really no limit to what you can put into budaejjigae. So don't be afraid to mix, match, and experiment!

Soak the rice cakes and sweet potato noodles separately in plenty of cold water for 30 minutes, then drain.

INGREDIENTS

8 ounces rice cakes
4 ounces dangmyun (sweet potato noodles)
6 cups water
10 large dried anchovies, cleaned and
   put in a strainer ball (page 97)
1 (4-inch-square) dashima (dried kelp)
6 dried shiitake mushrooms
3 hot dogs
1/2 (12-ounce) can Spam
8 ounces firm tofu
1 (3 1/2-ounce) package fresh enoki mushrooms
3 green onions, white and green parts
2 cups kimchi (page 26)
2 tablespoons gochujang (red chile paste)
1 tablespoon Korea red chile flakes
1 tablespoon soy sauce
2 teaspoons sugar
1/2 (14-ounce) can baked beans, drained
1 (4.2-ounce) package ramen

Meanwhile...

Let's make the broth! Boil the water with dried anchovies, dashima, and dried shiitake mushrooms for 30 minutes.

Cut the hot dogs, Spam, and tofu into 1/2-inch-thick, bite-size pieces.

DISCARD

Wash the enoki mushrooms and discard the roots. Cut the green onions into 1-inch pieces.

Cut the kimchi into bite-size pieces.

In a small bowl, mix the chile paste, chile flakes, soy sauce, sugar, and the packet of seasoning from the ramen.

Arrange the tofu, Spam, hot dogs, baked beans, rice cake, and kimchi in the bottom of a pot. Put the sweet potato noodles and the ramen noodles on top.

Strain the broth and discard the anchovies, dashima and shiitake mushrooms. Pour the sauce mixture and the remaining broth into the pot and boil it for 5 to 10 minutes, until the rice cake and noodles are al dente.

Last...

Add the green onions and enoki mushrooms and boil for a couple of minutes. Now, it's ready to eat!

Make it Deluxe!

You can easily make a deluxe version of budaejjigae by adding any of these ingredients:

Fresh chiles if you like it more spicy.

Diced ham for more meat.

A slice of American cheese melted on top at the last minute for richer flavor!

Soybean sprouts for more fiber.

ENJOY!

Seafood & Green Onion Pancake

(Haemul Pajeon)

This delicious pancake is usually served piping hot right out of the pan with a dipping sauce. It goes great with the Korean rice wine called makgeolli.

Cooking time: 30 minutes   Makes 4 to 6 servings

INGREDIENTS

1 cup all-purpose flour
1 egg
Salt
$1^1/_3$ cups water
4 green onions, white and green parts
2 cups frozen seafood mix, defrosted
2 tablespoons olive oil

- -

Dipping Sauce
2 tablespoons soy sauce
1 tablespoon rice vinegar
1 tablespoon sugar
1 teaspoon toasted sesame seeds
1 teaspoon Korean red chile flakes
2 tablespoons water

Let's make the batter!

Mix the flour, egg, and a pinch of salt with the water.

Cut the green onions into 2-inch pieces and halve the thicker pieces to even out the thickness.

Coat a large nonstick pan with 2 tablespoons olive oil and heat it over high heat. Pour a scoop of the batter into the pan, then reduce the heat to medium.

Evenly place the green onions and seafood on top and cover them with another ladleful of the batter.

Press the pancake
with a spatula to
make sure everything
lies flat and even,
then leave it to cook
for about 5 minutes.

When the edges start to brown, lift
with a spatula to check the bottom.
If the pancake is golden brown,
flip it and cook the other side.

Tips on Flipping

First, jerk the pan to make sure
the pancake is not stuck on the
bottom of the pan and that it
has formed a solid crust.

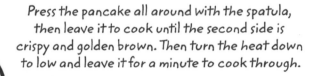

Then make a
quick flip as
you slightly tilt
the pan.

Drizzle a bit more oil
around the edges and
shake the pan to get
the oil to spread out
under the pancake.

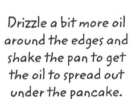

Press the pancake all around with the spatula,
then leave it to cook until the second side is
crispy and golden brown. Then turn the heat down
to low and leave it for a minute to cook through.

THE Dipping Sauce

Mix the soy sauce,
vinegar, sugar, sesame
seeds, and red chile
flakes with water.

Transfer the pancake to a
serving plate and slice it into
pieces for easy sharing!

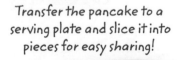

ENJOY

KIMCHI·PANCAKE

(Kimchi Buchimgae)

Buchimgae means pancake in Korean, and there are dozens of different kinds. This is a great way to use up leftover napa cabbage kimchi. You can make it with just flour, water, and kimchi, but I like to add ground pork for a richer flavor.

Cooking time: 30 minutes Makes 4 to 6 servings

Old kimchi preferred.

Optional

INGREDIENTS

1 cup all-purpose flour
1 cup water
1/3 cup kimchi juice
1 1/2 cups kimchi (page 26)
1 Korean green chile pepper (optional)
1/4 cup ground pork
Olive oil

First!

In a mixing bowl, whisk together the flour, water, and kimchi juice until there are no clumps.

Cut the kimchi into small pieces. If you want it extra spicy, cut a green chile pepper into thin rings too.

Then mix the kimchi, ground pork, and green chile into the batter.

Tip:
You can substitute any meat for the ground pork, including canned tuna or even oysters!

Heat up a large nonstick pan with plenty of oil over high heat. Pour one big ladelful of the batter in it. Quickly spread the batter evenly with a ladle or spatula and reduce the heat to medium. Leave it to cook for about 5 minutes.

PUSH

Tik Tok

When the bottom of the pancake has formed a golden brown crust, flip it with a spatula.

OIL

Chrr..

Drizzle a bit more oil around the edges and shake the pan to spread the oil. Cook the pancake until the second side is crispy. Then turn the heat down to low and leave it for a minute to cook through.

Transfer the pancake to a serving plate and cut it into easy-to-share pieces.

Let's eat!

A cold beer or makgeolli (unfiltered rice wine) goes great with this dish!

ENJOY

Chapter 10
Korean Fusion

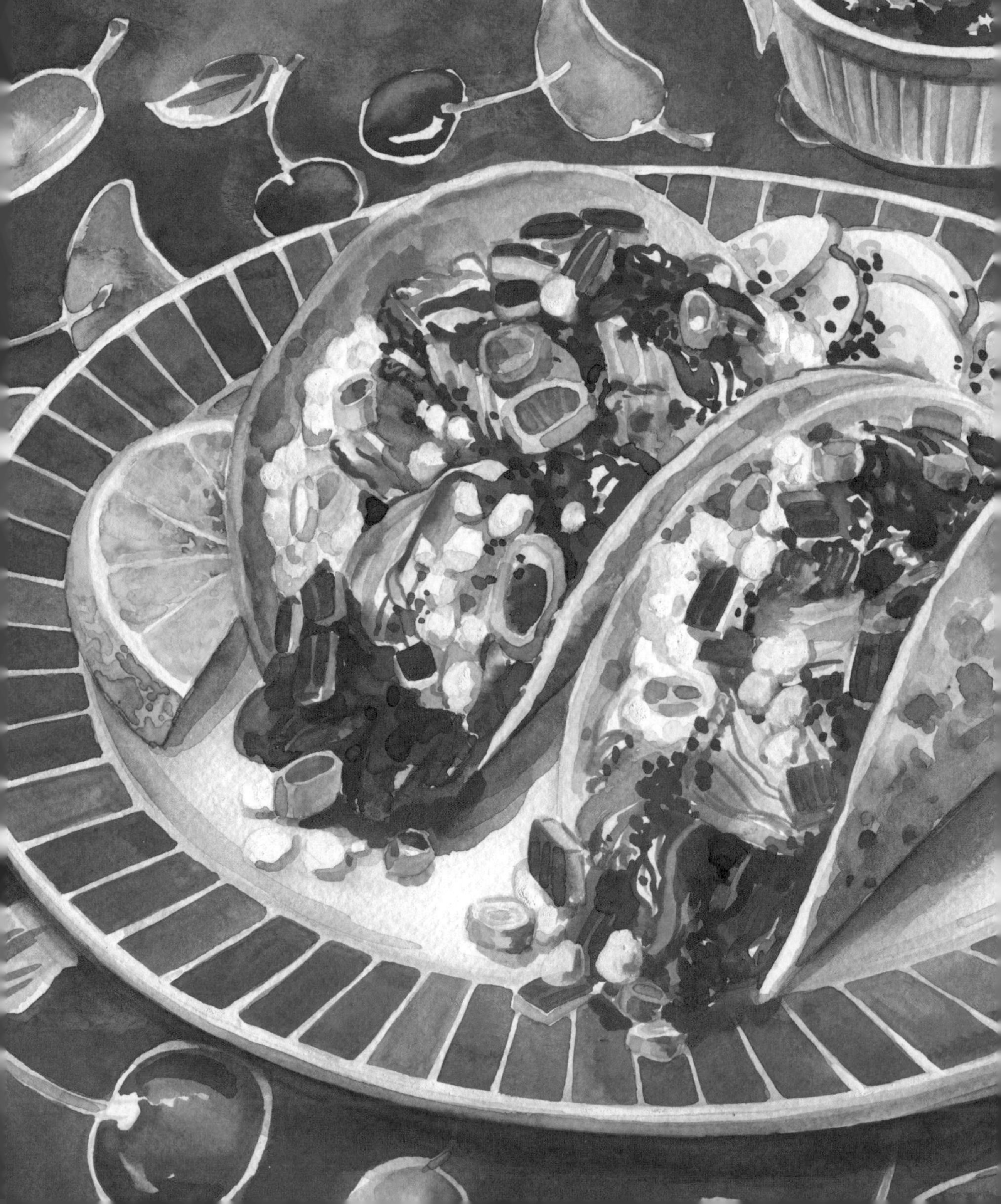

INTRO TO FOREIGN FOOD IN KOREA

I DON'T WANNA BE All BY MY~ SEeEELF

Korea is isolated by mountains and the sea from our only neighbors, China and Japan.

It was not until in the twentieth century that Korea got a chance to taste foreign flavors.

Korean-Chinese metal take-out box.

Black soybean noodles

Sweet-and-sour pork

好!

Chinese immigrants introduced their noodles, sauces, and frying techniques, developing a unique culinary fusion in Korea.

Chinese food also crossed over to Japan and then to Korea as noodle dishes such as jjamppong, ramen, and udon.

Japan opened its gates to the world early on and had adopted flavors from all over the world, including America.

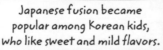

Japanese fusion became popular among Korean kids, who like sweet and mild flavors.

With Korean enthusiasm for world tourism growing over the past thirty years, many foreign cuisines have made their way into Korea.

Now you can easily find many international restaurants in Korea.

Korean food has also become popular in the States in recent years.

I put kimchi in everything these days.

It's on every blog too.

Oh, I've seen this truck on TV!

You can find Korean food trucks in most cities and kimchi in many American supermarkets now.

Adding kimchi or Korean chile paste is an easy way to kick any meal up a notch.

Korean barbecue sauce is great for any meat dish.

Experiment and explore your own fusion with Korean flavors!

Omelet (Omurice)
FRIED RICE

Omurice is a nickname for omelet fried rice. It is basically fried rice smothered in ketchup and wrapped in an omelet. It is said to have originated in Tokyo around the turn of the twentieth century and then spread throughout Asia. It is a staple of Korean kids' menus because of its bright, cute plating and mildly sweet and tangy flavor.

Cooking time: 30 minutes   Makes 3 servings

INGREDIENTS

8 ounces boneless, skinless
   chicken thighs
1/2 medium yellow onion
1 small carrot
Olive oil
1 teaspoon soju (Korean rice liquor)
Salt
Freshly ground pepper
1/2 cup sweet peas* (see next page)
1/2 cup sweet corn* (see next page)
3 cups freshly cooked rice
   (see page 18)
2 tablespoons butter
1/4 cup ketchup, plus more
   for serving
1 tablespoon soy sauce

- - - - - - - - - - - - - - - - - - - -

Omelets
6 eggs
3 tablespoons milk
3 tablespoons water
Salt
Fresh parsley leaves, for garnish

You can use any type of meat you want but I use chicken here. First, cut away the fat on the chicken and cut the chicken into small bite-size pieces.

Wash and peel the carrot and peel the onion. Dice them into tiny pieces.

Heat up a wok with a tablespoon of oil and sauté the chicken with soju, a pinch of salt, pepper, and onion for a couple of minutes, until the chicken is no longer pink.

*You can use fresh, canned, or frozen sweet peas and corn. If you are using canned vegetables, drain the liquid.

Add the carrot, sweet peas, and corn to the wok and sauté for a minute. Then add the rice, butter, and a pinch of salt and pepper and mix well. Sauté until all the liquid from the vegetables is absorbed by the rice. Then mix in the ketchup and soy sauce and remove from the heat.

For the omelets, whisk the eggs with the milk, water and a pinch of salt.

Heat up a pan with 2 teapoons of oil over medium heat and and pour in a third of the egg mixture.

Cook for a couple of minutes and flip over to cook the other side. Repeat and make two more omelets.

Drape each omelet in a bowl and scoop in the fried rice. Fold the edges of the omelet over the rice.

Flip!

TADA!

Put a plate over the bowl and flip it with both hands to invert the omelet-covered rice ball onto the plate.

ENJOY

Squirt some extra ketchup into a fun shape and garnish with parsley. Now it's ready to eat!

Sweet & Sour Pork (Tangsuyuk)

This Korean-Chinese dish bursts with a medley of flavors—sweet, sour, salty, and savory. And the double frying makes the pork strips superyummy and crispy.

Prep time: overnight Cooking time: 1 hour Makes 4 to 6 servings

INGREDIENTS

1 cup plus 3 tablespoons cornstarch
1 ounce dried wood ear mushrooms*
1½ pounds pork sirloin
5 cloves garlic, crushed
½ tablespoon salt
½ tablespoon freshly ground pepper
1 teaspoon toasted sesame oil
½ large cucumber, unpeeled
1 small yellow onion
½ yellow bell pepper
1 cup canned sliced pineapple
1 egg white
5 cups refined corn oil, for frying
Pickled yellow radish, for side dish

Sauce
8 tablespoons sugar
6 tablespoons white vinegar
2 tablespoons ketchup
2 tablespoons oyster sauce
2 tablespoons soy sauce
3 tablespoons water

Whisk 1 cup of the cornstarch with 1 cup of water and set aside overnight at room temperature.

CORN STARCH

WOOD EAR
MUSHROOMS

*Wood ear mushrooms are also called elephant ear mushrooms. You can find them at Chinese, Korean and some health food stores.

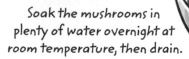

Soak the mushrooms in plenty of water overnight at room temperature, then drain.

Cut the pork into ½-inch-thick, 2-inch-long slices.

Mix the pork strips with the garlic, salt, pepper, and toasted sesame oil and set aside in the refrigerator for 30 minutes.

DISCARD

Cut the cucumber into ¼-inch, half-moons and cut away the seeds.

Cut the onion and bell pepper into 1-inch squares.

Drain the liquid from the canned pineapple and cut it into bite-size pieces.

Carefully discard the water that has floated above the cornstarch you've set aside overnight.

Then...

Add the egg white to the soaked cornstarch and mix well. Coat the pork strips well with the egg white—cornstarch batter.

Time for frying!

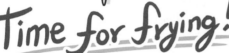

Heat up 5 cups of oil in a wok—enough for deep-frying.

Stick in a wooden chopstick to see if the oil is hot enough—if bubbles form around the chopstick, it's ready.

Chrr...

Drop the pork strips into the oil one by one, so they don't clump together. Fry for 20 seconds, until they turn golden brown. Take the strips out of the wok with chopsticks and drain the excess oil on paper towels. In the same oil, quickly fry at once the cucumber, onion, and bell pepper for 5 seconds and drain the excess oil on paper towels. Remove the wok from the heat; you'll use the oil again.

Let's make the SAUCE!

Mix the sugar, vinegar, ketchup, oyster sauce, and soy sauce in a saucepan and set over high heat. Bring to a boil and add the pineapple and wood ear mushrooms.

In a small bowl, whisk the remaining 3 tablespoons of cornstarch with 3 tablespoons of water and add it to the saucepan. Reduce the heat to low and stir until the sauce becomes gooey.

Reheat the oil in the wok until bubbles form around a chopstick and then flash-fry the pork strips for 20 seconds. Drain the excess oil on paper towels and serve it with the fried vegetables; pour the sauce on top.

A side of pickled yellow radish.

ENJOY

Black Soybean Noodles

(Jjajangmyeon)

Jjajangmyeon is probably the most popular Korean-Chinese dish in Korea. I have never seen it served at Chinese restaurants. It is only available at Korean-Chinese restaurants. The name jjajang comes from chujang, which is the Chinese black soybean sauce. You can use shrimp and squid instead of pork. You can also eat it with freshly cooked rice instead of noodles.

Cooking time: 30 minutes Makes 2 or 3 servings

INGREDIENTS

1 medium yellow potato
1 small onion
1/2 medium zucchini
8 ounces pork shoulder
7 tablespoons jjajang powder
2 cups water
2 tablespoons toasted sesame oil
1 teaspoon soju (Korean rice liquor)
2 (8-ounce) bundles jjajang noodles*
1 cucumber, cut into thin matchsticks
Danmuji (pickled yellow radish),
   for garnish

Jjajangmyeon is so popular in Korea that there are dozens of different kinds of readymade sauces and noodles available at Korean grocery stores to make it.

I'm using jjajang powder for this recipe, which already has the cornstarch mixed in.

3 1/2 tablespoons of jjajang powder mixed with 1 cup of water makes about 1 serving of the sauce.

Jjajang noodles are thick and round like udon noodles. You can find the noodles in the refrigerated section of Korean grocery stores.

Wash all the veggies and peel the potato and onion. Trim the fat off the pork. Cut the potato, onion, zucchini and pork into about 1/2-inch cubes.

In a bowl, mix the jjajang powder with 1 cup of the water and set aside.

Time to WOK OUT!

Heat up 1 tablespoon sesame oil in a wok over high heat and sauté the pork with the soju until the pork is no longer pink. Add the potato and sauté it for a minute, then add the onion, zucchini, and jjajang and water.

Get 'em All~

After you've poured in the jjajang and water, add the remaining 1 cup of water to the same bowl, swish it around to pick up all of the powder residue, and pour that into the wok.

1 cup water

Stir everything well and turn down the heat to medium. Stir occasionally so the sauce doesn't stick to the bottom and cook until the potato becomes soft, about 10 minutes.

THE NOODLES

Take out the bundles of noodles . . .

. . . and loosen up the strands on a plate.

Put the noodles in a boiling pot of water . . .

. . . for about 6 minutes.

TIPS

Cut a noodle to see if it is cooked through.

If there's no hard white center, it's done!

SESAME OIL

Drain the noodles and toss them with 1 tablespoon of toasted sesame oil. The oil makes the noodles easy to mix with the sauce.

Put the noodles in a serving bowl and pour the pork and vegetable mixture on top. Garnish with thinly sliced cucumber. Serve with pickled yellow radish.

ENJOY

Spicy Chicken Tacos

(Buldak Taco)

Mexican food is quite similar to Korean food—both use a lot of rice and spicy chile sauces and put their food in wraps. I love tacos because you can combine any fillings you like in a tortilla, similar to how Koreans eat grilled meat wrapped in lettuce. You can substitute pork or beef for the chicken in this recipe.

Cooking time: 40 minutes Makes 4 to 6 servings

Remove the excess fat from the chicken thighs and cut the chicken into small bite-size pieces.

Let's make the marinade!

Peel the onion, garlic, and ginger and cut them into small pieces. Then blend them with the soy sauce, sesame oil, and soju.

Blend in the chile paste, chile flakes, sugar, and pepper.

INGREDIENTS

3 pounds boneless, skinless chicken thighs
1 small yellow onion
6 cloves garlic
1 (1/2-inch) piece fresh ginger
2 tablespoons soy sauce
1 tablespoon toasted sesame oil
1 tablespoon soju (Korean rice liquor)
3 tablespoons gochujang (red chile paste)
1 tablespoon Korean red chile flakes
1 tablespoon sugar
1 teaspoon freshly ground pepper

Kimchi Salsa
2 medium tomatoes
1/2 cup kimchi (page 26)
2 green onions, white and green parts
3 tablespoons finely chopped fresh cilantro
Juice of 1/2 lime
1 teaspoon olive oil
1 teaspoon fish sauce
Freshly ground pepper

Tacos and Toppings
1 avocado, sliced into thin wedges
12 tortillas or taco shells (flour or corn)
1 cup shredded iceberg lettuce
1 cup crumbled queso fresco
1/2 cup sour cream

Caliente~♡

In a bowl, pour the marinade over the chicken and mix well by hand. Cover it with a lid or plastic wrap and set aside in the refrigerator for 30 minutes.

30 minutes Later...

Sauté the marinated chicken over high heat for 5 to 10 minutes, until the meat is fully cooked.

The Kimchi SALSA

Make the salsa while the chicken is marinating. Dice the tomato and kimchi into small bite-size cubes. Slice the green onions into thin rings. Put the veggies in a bowl and mix them well with the cilantro, lime juice, olive oil, fish sauce, and a pinch of freshly ground pepper.

Warm up the tortillas in a pan over low heat for a minute before serving. Wrap them in a cloth to keep them warm.

fiesta!

ENJOY!

169

KOREAN BURGERS
(Kimchi Galbi Burger)

Galbi marinade can amp up the umami flavor of any burger or steak. Korean condiments can also add a kick to common Western sauces like ketchup and mayonnaise.
Cooking time: 50 minutes Makes 6 servings

> Let's make the marinade. Peel and chop the onion, garlic, and ginger into small pieces and blend them with the soy sauce, soju, sugar, pepper, and sesame oil in a food processor.

~wee

INGREDIENTS

Burgers
1 small yellow onion
6 cloves garlic
1 (1/2-inch) piece fresh ginger
3 tablespoons soy sauce
1 tablespoon soju (Korean rice liquor)
1 tablespoon sugar
1 teaspoon freshly ground pepper
1 teaspoon toasted sesame oil
2 pounds lean ground beef
1 egg
6 toasted sesame burger buns
6 slices cheese (optional)
Korean Fusion Condiments
 (see sidebar)
Romaine lettuce, for serving (optional)

- - - - - - - - - - - - - - - - - -

Kimchi Spread
2 cups kimchi (page 26)
1 small yellow onion
1 tablespoon butter

In a bowl, use your hands to mix the ground beef with the marinade and egg.

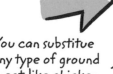

You can substitue any type of ground meat, like chicken or pork.

Divide the meat into six portions and form into patties.

Wrap the patties individually in plastic wrap and refrigerate for 30 minutes.

The Kimchi Spread

Drain the liquid from the kimchi and cut the kimchi into small bite-size pieces.

Peel the onion and dice it into small bite-size cubes.

In a pan over high heat, sauté the onion and kimchi in the butter for about 5 minutes, until the onion turns semitranslucent.

On a grill or stovetop, cook the beef patties to the desired doneness and melt the cheese slices on top.

Toast the buns before serving.

Slather the condiments of your choice on the toasted buns and put on some lettuce and a beef patty and top it with kimchi spread.

Yum!

KOREAN FUSION CONDIMENTS

For dipping French fries or slathering on burger buns and hot dogs, these are AWESOME SAUCES!

Spicy Caviar Mayonnaise

Mix 1/2 cup mayonnaise, 1/2 tablespoon gochujang (red chile paste) and 2 tablespoons tobiko (flying fish roe).

You can find flying fish roe in the fresh seafood section at Korean and Japanese grocery stores.

Soy Sesame Mayonnaise

Mix 1/2 cup of mayonnaise, 1 teaspoon of toasted sesame seeds, 1 teaspoon of soy sauce, 1 teaspoon of toasted sesame oil, and 1 tablespoon of thinly sliced green onion.

Sweet & Spicy Ketchup

Mix 1/4 cup ketchup with 1/4 cup gochujang (red chile paste) and 1 tablespoon honey.

ENJOY!

Acknowledgments

I grew up in Korea until I was fourteen years old. My mom raised me alone.

Wear this and eat this.

OK.

Korean kids are raised to always obey their parents and never question. My mom was the only influence and authority in my childhood. I ate, thought, and acted just like her.

Then we moved to the United States.

Mom, when are we coming back?

Umm... Actually, we aren't coming back.

WHAT?!

Why can't you just get a real 9-to-5 job at a big, secure company? And you shouldn't live in Brooklyn, it's too dirty and dangerous!

I want to be a cartoonist and I like Brooklyn. Why can't you just accept that?

I've lived apart from her since college. As a 1.5 generation Korean-American, my tastes and opinions became quite different from my mom's.

I'd never spent much time cooking with my mom until I started working on this book. I realized cooking with Mom can be an emotional roller coaster. During the countless hours we spent together in the kitchen in the past eight months, we've learned a lot about each other, from what flavors we like to what ticks the other off. Mothers and daughters pushing each other's buttons are quite common. Our struggles just got more intense sometimes because of our cultural differences and because I'm the only daughter of a single mother.

Mother and daughter cooking together in the media.

Who ARE these people?!

The real-life mother and daughter cooking together.

Ginger shouldn't go in this dish, and it needs more soy sauce!

I like ginger, so back off!

CLANK

ROAR!

Poor ginger

SMASH!

WOOSH

My mom is my toughest critic, in the way that Korean mothers can be.

You've cut this too thick.

Hmm, this does need more soy sauce.

Sneak in

SOY SAUCE

Whatever disagreement we've had in the kitchen, I know her criticisms made my food better.

She went above and beyond to help me write sixty-four recipes for this book, from grocery shopping to cooking, tasting and eating the leftovers with me.

This is how you clean squid.

Eww, gross!

SPLUG

I could never have finished this book without her help. This book is the product of her effort as much as mine. I thank my mom from the bottom of my heart.

I put in some ginger this time.

OK.

I love you, mom.

We find it so difficult to say "I love you" out loud to each other. Maybe we are too tough, shy, or stubborn. Or maybe those words just can't contain all of our feelings.

Index

Copyright © 2016 by Robin Ha
Illustrations copyright © 2016 by Robin Ha

Many of these recipes appeared in an earlier format
on the author's blog "Banchan in 2 Pages."

Published in the United States by Ten Speed Press,
an imprint of the Crown Publishing Group, a division
of Penguin Random House LLC, New York.

www.crownpublishing.com
www.tenspeed.com

Ten Speed Press and the Ten Speed Press colophon are
registered trademarks of Penguin Random House LLC.

Library of Congress Cataloging-in-Publication Data
Ha, Robin, author.
Cook Korean! : a comic book with recipes / Robin Ha.
Berkeley : Ten Speed Press, 2016. I Includes bibliographical
references and index.
LCSH: Cooking, Korean—Comic books, strips, etc. I
BISAC: COOKING /
  Regional & Ethnic / Asian. I COMICS & GRAPHIC NOVELS /
Nonfiction. I
  COOKING / Regional & Ethnic / General. I
LCGFT: Cookbooks. I Comics
  (Graphic works)
Classification: LCC TX724.5.K65 H2355 2016 (print) I
LCC TX724.5.K65
(ebook)
  I DDC 641.59519—dc23

Trade Paperback ISBN: 978-1-6077-4887-8
eBook ISBN: 978-1-6077-4888-5

Printed in China

Design by Chloe Rawlins

10 9

First Edition